PARADISE TEMPLE

www.royalcollins.com

PARADISE TEMPLE

A Selection of Lu Min's
Short Stories

LU MIN

Books Beyond Boundaries

ROYAL COLLINS

Paradise Temple: A Selection of Lu Min's Short Stories

Lu Min

First published in 2021 by Royal Collins Publishing Group Inc.
Groupe Publication Royal Collins Inc.
BKM Royalcollins Publishers Private Limited

Headquarters: 550-555 boul. René-Lévesque O Montréal (Québec) H2Z1B1 Canada
India office: 805 Hemkunt House, 8th Floor, Rajendra Place, New Delhi 110 008

Original Edition © Nanjing Normal University Press was included in the series
"A Bilingual Library Contemporary Chinese Master Writers", edited by Yang
Haocheng and Li Zhongtao.

This English edition is authorized by Nanjing Normal University Press.

ISBN: 978-1-4878-0810-5

To find out more about our publications, please visit www.royalcollins.com

PREFACE

Do college students read today? Certainly they do, but what do they read? They surf the net, they read text messages, and they get bogged down in an ocean of information from blogs or WeChat. They seem to read extensively, but much they read and enjoy reading is nothing but sheer guff and hogwash. They know something about everything, but nothing they know seems to be of any substantial depth or breadth. With their mobile phones constantly in their hands at every moment, they are phubbing all those around them. The tiny machine makes its way to the classroom, where it replaces the textbook as the most eye-catching and attention-drawing plaything to the hopeless stare of the teachers. "The textbook is full of corrupt stuff anyway," I recall with astonishment my late advisor Jessie Chambers saying years ago, when she was asked to give her opinion on China's college education.

So it is fragmented reading from the new media that college students seem to be enjoying today, and serious literature is woefully slighted or neglected, forgotten in the dust-covered shelves of the libraries, becoming spiritual food for a minority of book-ish souls. When it comes to English learning, the situation is no more encouraging. Chinese students do not read serious literature anymore. What they have learned is gibberish full of "kind of," or internet jive and cants, some pop songs, and an exaggerated show of shrugs. They count themselves fluent in English, not knowing that a real command of the foreign tongue is built on an extensive reading of good literature of all kinds.

Talking of extracurricular reading, I remember what I saw when my wife and I visited her cousin eleven years ago in New York. She had a son and a daughter. The boy, Franklin, was an undergraduate of the University of Pennsylvania, and the girl, Shelly, having just finished her elementary school, was awaiting with great excitement her commencement, which we all attended the next day. Out of curiosity, I flipped through Shelly's reading materials. I saw Shakespeare, Milton, Mark Twain, Hemingway, and other renowned writers lying helter-skelter on her reading table. There was also a copy of *Harry Potter*, of course. I asked Shelly, "You're reading these?" "Yes, for fun!" she snapped. An elementary school pupil reading Shakespeare, Milton, Mark Twain, and Hemingway outside the classroom! And for fun! What are our college students reading? This question has weighed upon me like a leaden slab over the years.

Maybe American students aren't a good comparison? Let's look instead, then, at the contents of Freshman Readings in English for undergraduate students at the National Southwestern Associated University in war-torn China. Mind you, this was for all the freshmen, not just those majoring in English. Compiled by Prof Chen Futian, a Hawaii-born Harvard ME, the Readings had a total of 43 essays, almost all written by master hands and which smack of a strong spirit of liberal education. The Readings were vastly different from the so-called "Practical English," "Business English," "Legal English," "Secretarial English," and other such courses prevalent in college classrooms today. They included "Barren Spring" by Pearl S. Buck, "Beast of Burden" and "Song of the River" by W. Somerset Maugham, "Birth of a Sister" by Tan Shih-hua, "A Dissertation upon Roast Pig" by Charles Lamb, "An Optimistic Look at China" by Hu Shih, "The End of Life" by Lin Yutang, "A Sacred Mountain" by G. Lowes Dickinson, "Fragments from a Flower Diary" by Nora Waln, "A Word to Youth" by Andre Maurois, "A Pair of Woodpeckers" by an unknown author, "The Battle of the Red and the Black Ants" by Henry David Thoreau, "Liberty" by Woodrow Wilson, "What Is Science?" by Ira Remsen, "The Durable Satisfactions of Life" by Charles W. Eliot, "The Imaginary Invalid" by Jerome K. Jerome, "The Tell-Tale Heart" by Edgar Allan Poe, "The Widow and Her Son" by Washington Irving, "The Champion Snorer" by an unknown author, "A Liberal Education" by Thomas Henry Huxley, "The Function of Education in Democratic Society" by Charles W. Eliot, "What Shall We Educate for?" by Bertrand Russell, "The Strength of Democracy" by Walter Lippmann, "Technological Civilization" by Charles A. Beard, "The Social Value of the College-Bred" by William James, "Liberty and Discipline" by Abbot Lawrence Lowell, "The Liberation of a People's Vital Energies" by Woodrow Wilson, "Habit" by William James, "Why a Classic is a Classic" by Arnold Bennett, "Evolution" by John Galsworthy, "Fighting in Gallipoli" by John Masefield, "The Half Mile" by T. O. Beachcroft, "The Long Shadow" by John Hampson, "The Field Where the Satyrs Danced" by Lord Dunsany, "Every Man's Natural Desire to Be Somebody Else" by Samuel McChord Crothers, "The Philosopher" by W. Somerset Maugham, "Bismarck" by Emil Ludwig, "The Riddle of Hitler" by Stephen H. Roberts, "British Foreign Policy" by John Gunther, "The American Love of Freedom" by Edmund Burke, "What is a University?" by John Henry Newman, "Theory of the Liberal College" by Alexander Meiklejohn, and "Self-Cultivation in English" by George Herbert Palmer. And these are just freshman readings. Just imagine what the students would be like after four years of intensive reading of arts and letters like these.

You would say that most of these are foreign literature, and our students are Chinese, and as Chinese they must be well versed in their mother tongue or well read in Chinese literature. Not at all! I find to my dismay that today's Chinese college students haven't read anything of Chinese literary classics. I used to teach a course entitled Translation of Literary Classics. Among all the English and Chinese materials I'd prepared, nothing seemed to have been on the students' reading list except perhaps Lu Xun's "Kong Yiji," which was in their middle school textbook. They're well acquainted with, say, the names of the "Four Literary Masterpieces," but not many of them have bothered to read any of them. Taoist and Confucian classics such as Daodejing (Classics of the Way and Virtue), *Zhuangzi, The Analects, Mencius, The Great Learning,* and *The Doctrine of the Golden Mean* were all must reads of any school kids in olden days, but today, they are even more out of the question. Today's students claim that their teachings are too far detached from real life and their mode of linguistic expression is miserably esoteric to modern readers.

This situation is discouraging enough, but it is against this gloomy background that A Bilingual Library of Contemporary Chinese Master Writers has been launched by Nanjing Normal University Press, in hopes of bringing back some of the lost lambs to the conventional mode of paper book reading. However, our target readers are not limited to college students, and anyone who might be interested in Chinese-English translation, comparative literature, and comparative studies between Chinese and Western cultures may find their own rewards in reading from the Library, for which there are two points to say at the least. First, the present Library was born amidst the favorable climate of Chinese culture Going Global which, as a top-down, nationwide, and now largely canonized slogan, was a significant factor in its publication. It is natural that when a country has earned a stronghold in the world economy, as China has now done so robustly, it will desire to go all out in other respects, including culture. Historically, it has been true of such institutions as the Alliance Française, the British Council, and the Goethe-Institut, all important channels for their respective countries' cultural flow and interaction. It is probably a matter of national self-confidence and pride, but there is nothing wrong with that. The question that remains is how a country's culture should go global. Two forces are at work: various bureaucrats, and professionals such as researchers, writers, translators, editors, and publishers. The two forces have the same aim, but sadly, each espouses different strategies and approaches for introducing their cultural achievements to the outside world. Largely ignorant of the foreign languages and their cultures, bureaucrats want very much to sell what they deem to be precious material to a potential buyer, not knowing that cultural exchange is, to a great extent, like trade and is built on the basis of equal give-and-take and willingness on the side of the buyer, while any one-sided forced selling is doomed to fail. Though much more informed, the professionals are reliant on the bureaucrats for political direction and financial support, and are thus left in a dilemma. They want to proceed with what they regard as the right path, but are frequently met with undesirable obstacles, including unwelcomed directions or interferences from the bureaucrats. The case of *Chinese Literature*, an officially sponsored magazine that has struggled for a full fifty years, is instructive. Though *CL* has had as its chief editor the prolific, charismatic translator Yang Xianyi for the second half of its fifty-year life, Yang alone certainly would not have had sufficient strength to stay clear of the political influences of his day. *CL* bears the clear hallmark of its time, which explains its low readership overseas over the years.

Fortunately, the present *Library* is able to adhere to its set standard, and what is collected here are either representative works or highly recognized pieces of some of the most famous writers from contemporary China. After the lapse of dozens of years of ideological struggles, we are able to return at last to the ontological study of literary creation, and all the works translated here speak of the commonality of human nature and human life – humankind's happiness, anger, sorrow, and joy – despite their vastly different approaches and perspectives toward literature. With their succinct style, exquisite structure, and typical characters and events, these stories constitute an extremely important, integral part of the treasure house of contemporary Chinese literature. For a better, more three-dimensional presentation of the authors and their works, we have also included a critique and an interview for each author, with only a few exceptions.

In addition, it is common knowledge among translators that they do better when translating into their mother tongue. It's an undeniable fact that translators whose mother tongue is English will be much more at home when it comes to Chinese-English translation. Professor Yang Haocheng used to call Sidney Shapiro about his translation of *Outlaws of the Marsh*. Mr. Shapiro once said to him on the phone, "Translating things like *Outlaws of the Marsh* is much easier for me than translating English materials into Chinese. After all, Chinese is not my mother tongue, though I became a Chinese citizen all the way back in 1963."

The present *Library* boasts a terrific pool of professional translators whose mother tongue is English, and all of them are bilingual or multilingual. They are the same translators who are working for *Chinese Arts & Letters*. This makes all the difference. In fact, both *Chinese Literature* and almost all other journals and magazines run by Chinese publishers have the same problem. Many of their translators are non-native speakers or writers of the target language, and their English was learned as a second language. They cannot be compared with professional translators whose mother tongue is English and, better still, whose command of the Chinese language is superb. Many of them are internationally recognized sinologists or old China hands to boot. Denis Mair, Nicky Harman, Natascha Bruce, Luisetta Mudie, Shelly Bryant, Josh Stenberg, Helen Wang, Jeremy Tiang, Eric Abrahamsen, Michael Day, Simon Patton, and Florence Woo are among our most conscientious and treasured translators. What comes out of their hands may seem at first glance to be nothing special, yet their work is so idiomatic and reads so comfortably that we cannot help but admire.

The target audience of the present *Library*, then, should first of all be readers interested in translation, especially undergraduates and graduate students studying translation. When Professor Yang Haocheng was reading the manuscripts prepared by these translators, he often could not keep himself from copying their wonderful translations with careful analysis, such as the rendering of, "她有着凹凸有致的身材" (meaning "she has a figure of voluptuous curves"). There is a special word, albeit highly colloquial, to describe that kind of girl, "zaftig." So we constantly hear people say, "She is a sort of zaftig, coquettish girl." Similarly, "包二奶" is a very common term today, and our translator renders it, "to keep a bit on the side." Accordingly, "当小三" is "to be somebody's bit on the side," "bit" meaning a loose woman, and "on the side," in secret or on the sly, but with a bit of humor. Likewise, "吃货," a term enjoyed by many young people today, has also its English equivalent, "greedy guts." (Mind you, it's *guts* and not *gut*. For instance: *He is a greedy guts.*) This is aside from other possible renderings, such as foodie, glutton, gourmand, gastronaut, or food aficionado, as listed by the most advanced Chinese-English Dictionary chief-edited by the late Professor Lu Gusun. And "恶搞" actually has a Japanese term "to kuso," which has already entered the English language, making "to parody," "to lampoon," and "to snark" seem somewhat outdated. "Phubber," the reverse formation of "phubbing," which is said to be a new coinage by some Australian linguists, lexicographers, and authors from "phone" and "snub," a neologism to describe the habit of snubbing people around you in favor of a mobile phone, is an exact equivalent of the the popular Chinese term "低头族." It only has a history of five years, and though already included in the Australian National Dictionary, most other dictionaries or thesauruses have not yet included it. And such simple oral sayings as "过了这村儿没这店儿" and "金窝银窝, 不如自家狗窝" are masterfully translated into the pithy phrase, "It's now or never," and the most faithful to date, "Gold dish, silver dish, they cannot compare to your own dog's dish," respectively, both genius outgrowths from the prosaic "last chance," and the equally memorable — though losing the image — clause, "East or west, home is best." This alone is a good reason why the *Library* is a good read for all who are interested in translation. In fact, editing these works has turned out to be a great opportunity for us editors to learn about the two languages, and it has generally uplifted us. Many universities have chosen the *Library* as the textbook for their translation courses and have included it in the list of reference books for the entrance examination for their Masters in Translation and Interpretation programs.

The target audience of *A Bilingual Library of Contemporary Chinese Master Writers* also includes scholars of comparative literature and comparative study of the cultures of East and West. With systematic planning, organization, and support, the quantity and quality of translations of Chinese literature have greatly improved. However, their influence overseas is still limited, and Chinese literature in translation is still not an "active presence" in World Literature. We believe that the key to addressing this problem is to emphasize not only international translation of Chinese literature, but also international literary criticism. At the Symposium on Chinese Literature Going Global since Mo Yan Won the Nobel Prize, Professor Song Binghui pointed out that "for Chinese literature to really go global, it must, to a large extent, depend on literary scholars' interpretation of the literary works, and having effective multiple interpretations of the literary works is an important factor in realizing the internationalization of local literature." When contemporary Chinese literature has been introduced to the world, this dimension has not received due attention, so we are trying to achieve a breakthrough in this area. After Professor Yang Haocheng passed away, we invited Professor Sheng Ning to be the editor-in-chief of *Chinese Arts & Letters*. Selection of the content for the *Library*, especially the interviews and criticisms, followed Professor Sheng Ning's suggestions. Professor Sheng Ning was formerly the editor-in-chief of *Foreign Literature Review*, the best journal in the field of foreign literature studies. On this platform, many Chinese scholars interpret and criticize foreign literature from various perspectives, facilitating the "active presence" of foreign literature in China. We hope that the *Library* will encourage scholars to criticize Chinese literature translated into English and as a part of World Literature. In other words, Professor Sheng Ning formerly focused on guiding scholars to criticize foreign literature in Chinese, but now he is focusing on guiding more scholars to criticize Chinese literature in foreign languages, including literary criticism from foreign sinologists. We hope to ensure that Chinese literature is not only effectively Going Global, but is also truly being appreciated.

A Bilingual Library of Contemporary Chinese Master Writers also aims to attract scholars' attention to the process of literary translation. As mentioned above, the translators of the *Library* are all sinologists whose mother tongue is English. At the same time, they collaborate with Chinese editors who are teachers from the

School of Foreign Languages and Cultures at Nanjing Normal University, specializing in literature or translation. The basic collaboration process involves the translator finishing the first draft and communicating with the editor whenever questions arise. After the first draft is finished, the editor proofreads it, then revises it with the translator. After the revision is completed, the editor-in-chief checks and approves the final draft. I am not a translation major, but from the time I began my job as editor at *Chinese Arts & Letters*, I was drawn to the various challenges that arose during this process. Although I knew little about translation theory, I could not wait to write an article entirely based on my own editing experience, "The Translator-Editor Collaboration in Translating Chinese Literature – Three Short Stories by Bi Feiyu as Case Studies". It has opened a new direction in my academic research, in which I have never lost interest. At present, *Chinese Arts & Letters* is setting up a Translation Process Corpus, and the materials in the translation process of *A Bilingual Library of Contemporary Chinese Master Writers* will be added to the Corpus as well. The Corpus will be open to all translation scholars to conduct studies from various perspectives and enrich the approaches to translation studies. The Translation Process Corpus showcases the communication between the translator who is a native speaker of English and the editor who is a native speaker of Chinese. They each exert their own mother tongue advantages, and interaction occurs between the two languages and cultures. They seek to make the translated text not only satisfy the target audience's reading habits and aesthetic preferences, but also convey the deepest cultural connotations of the original text. We may even imagine that if these materials crystalizing human intelligence in the translation field were "fed" in the proper way into an artificial intelligence and became deep-learning materials for AI, AI would one day translate every subtlety of the language with delicacy and beauty, breaking the bottleneck in AI translation.

Though, as mentioned earlier, the target audience of these works is relatively professional, we hope that the present *Library* will suit both refined and popular tastes and be put beside the pillows of all readers who are interested in literature. Professor Yang Haocheng once criticized young people today for being interested only in cellphones instead of books, saying, "So it is fragmented reading from the new media that college students seem to be enjoying today, and serious literature is woefully slighted or neglected, forgotten in the dust-covered shelves of the libraries, becoming the spiritual food for a minority of bookish souls." He hoped *A Bilingual Library of Contemporary Chinese Master Writers* would bring back some of "the lost lambs to the normal track of conventional paper book reading." I don't think I myself have the right to criticize young people today. Although I am not young, I read my cellphone much more frequently than I read paper books, which makes me one of "the lost lambs" criticized by Professor Yang Haocheng. But it is our hope that the *Library* will change our reading habits a little. If we plan to spend some time every day reading books, the short stories in *A Bilingual Library of Contemporary Chinese Master Writers* are an ideal starting point. As Su Tong, one of the writers introduced in Volume One of the *Library*, once said, "Short stories are like bedtime stories for adults, preferably being read beside the lamp, one piece per night. They can be tasted for three or five minutes, moving, amusing, depressing, or overwhelming the reader. If you experience these feelings, it shows that this short period of time has not been wasted. A habit like this ensures that each day will end in magnificence. How wonderful it is!" The *Library* contains wonderful short stories in both Chinese and English, which, we believe, will surely bring readers double happiness and growth.

Literary critic Wu Yiqin, academic and translator Xu Jun, and writer Su Tong have all voiced their strong support for this *Library*, each speaking from their different perspectives. These three are all towering figures in their own fields, and their opinions add to the authority of the *Library*.

This *Library* is meant to be open ended, though it is set to be developed on a five-author basis, which includes five short stories alongside a critique and an interview for each author, with slight variations in each issue. Various people have contributed their effort and lent their support to the publication of the *Library*, including our terrific translators, authors, critics, editors from *CAL* and Nanjing Normal University Press, and the Press's leadership, so you may say it's a joyful, well-orchestrated tutti.

YANG HAOCHENG

CONTENTS

XIE BOMAO
— R.I.P.

Translated by **Helen Wang**

I

Another letter arrived for Xie Bomao. The neatly written characters — in a small, regular script written with brush and ink — were instantly recognizable. And there, as always, were the same four characters at the bottom of the envelope: *Sent by Chen, Nanjing.*

Li Fu held it in his hand and stared at it. These letters troubled him. He tossed it carefully into the pigeonhole on the left, where he reckoned there must be another twenty, maybe thirty, dead letters addressed to Xie Bomao, all from this same person. Some were due for disposal, but Li Fu wouldn't let anyone touch them. He hadn't given up hope yet.

A "dead letter" was one that can't be delivered, forwarded or returned, either because the name and address wasn't clear or because there was some other kind of problem. The technical term was "undeliverable mail," which was as good as saying they were dead. All the dead letters in this city came here, to Li Fu, and his job was to try to rescue them. He'd been a postman for almost thirty years, and in the 1980s, during the flood of Taiwanese and overseas Chinese searching for relatives on the mainland, he'd rescued countless dead letters. His delivery section had been festooned with silk banners presented by tottering old folk, spreading even into the corridor leading to the toilets, covering every inch of the wall. He was elected a Provincial Level Model Worker, and his current position of "Letter Rescuer" had been created specifically for him, with the dual intention of using his expertise and of looking after him in his old age.

It was Li Fu's habit to carry a small notebook around with him, and to record in it his search for each letter — how many leads he had got and where each of them ended up, which household registration officer he had sought at which police station, which streets he had visited, and which people he had questioned. Over the years he had filled more than ten notebooks. He was still doing it now. As soon as he came across anyone who looked as though they might know something, he'd take his notebook out of his little green bag, look the person in the eye, and try to get to the bottom of the dubious address. In the 80s, his sense of purpose had been very touching, but by the 90s, it was almost painful to witness, and now, well, it was pathetic to see such tenacity over some dead letters. Even he found it difficult to explain. Perhaps it was just the postman in him. He'd probably throw himself into his work whatever he was. Lottery ticket seller, bike repairman, or cook, he'd be much the same.

Li Fu treated his dead letters with more care than a top surgeon might afford the terminally ill, and it was a shame the dead letters that had been placed in his hands these last few years had become increasingly ridiculous. All too often, the envelopes were printed or had transparent windows and were items of bulk mail franked Postage Paid, containing a random letter confirming admission to some private school, a VIP card for a beauty salon, a survey from a tourism website, or some other junk mail. Eighty to ninety per cent had false names or incorrect addresses, and even if he went to a great deal of trouble to find them, he could forget about a silk banner or a thank you. He'd be lucky if people opened the door and were polite enough to wait until he'd left before tossing the letter into the bin. He told himself not to mind — after all, when a doctor saves someone's life, there's no guarantee that the patient won't go and kill himself, is there?

And so, the first time he saw one of these letters — addressed to "Xie Bomao, 21 Bamboo Lattice Lane, Qinhuai District, Nanjing 210006. Sent by Chen, Nanjing" — and saw those exquisite characters, written with such mastery, on what was clearly a genuinely worthwhile personal letter, Li Fu the Letter Rescuer was overcome with emotion, with a surge of gratitude quite disproportionate to his job description. He'd spent all those years, a lifetime, in the company of letters, and now his very last search promised at least to be enjoyable, and maybe even rewarding. Li Fu worked his way through his entire checklist — the local administration office, the police station, the street, the residents' committee, and the residents who'd lived there longest. He checked the spelling of every personal name and every place name, and he tried substituting the characters with new ones that looked or sounded the same. His efforts were met with curiosity, with indifference, with impatience, with a shake of the head, or with a nonchalant sneer in his face. But Li Fu didn't care. Everything he tried was recorded in his notebook with the same diligence of the previous thirty years. And he was careful not to reveal his personal judgement — that all signs showed that these letters sent to Xie Bomao were indeed terminally ill and there was no hope of recovery.

So it came as a surprise and a shock when another dead letter to Xie Bomao arrived in his office about two weeks later, the first letter still unresolved. And after that, the small, regular characters written with brush and ink continued to arrive at an interval of two or three weeks, with one impossible address after another — One-Hundred-Cats Square, Mr Qin-the-Top Scholar's Lane, Welcome-the-Flute Port, The Gallery of Gems and Treasures, The Temple of Peace and Pleasure, Oil-Market Avenue, Sweeping-the-Petals House. Was this person called Chen leading him on a wild goose chase? Or was he desperately searching for a person with no fixed abode?

II

Xie Bomao was Chen Yixin's friend.

"Friend" is a widely-used, tricky word. When we're little, we're called "my little friend," to TV presenters we're "our friends in the audience," in shopping centers we're "our friends, the customers," and to strangers we're "my new found friends." And how often do we talk about going to watch a football match, or to have tea, with "a friend"? Even if we are defrauding or taking advantage of each other, we are still "business friends." Youths on the street will slap "a friend" on the shoulder before getting into a fight. Then, of course, there's sex and boyfriends and girlfriends. Oh, and I almost forgot about "old friends," like those famous "old friends" Chiang Kai-shek and Mao Zedong. And so it goes on.

All told, Chen Yixin had rather a lot of friends.

But Xie Bomao was a special friend, thanks to his five-year-old daughter. She had an invisible friend, though he couldn't see this friend and didn't know if it was human or not, male or female, or how old it was. What he did know was that she called it Flying Fish, and that he envied their intimacy. When she had her yoghurt drink, got up after sleeping, played with her toys, went to kindergarten, went to the washroom, or walked round the zoo, she would whisper and share her feelings with Flying Fish.

Then one day, a devil of an idea struck him. In the middle of his afternoon nap, he opened his eyes and saw the curtains fluttering, casting deathly shadows on the sofa. Two colleagues were giggling at something online across the room. There were bursts of excitement from the card players next door. There were some unread messages on his mobile, probably his wife checking to ask who was picking up their daughter from the kindergarten or some company promoting financial products. On QQ, his classmates, workmates, and hometown groups flashed endlessly. On Weibo, a stream of new messages rolled down the screen. Everything was like it always was, friendly bits of mediocrity bobbing about the world, like islands in the drift – then his mind suddenly filled with a childish desire. *I want a Flying Fish too.* He wanted a friend who no one else could see, a friend who would always know what he was feeling and would always be there with him.

Xie Bomao. The name came to him as he twisted himself off the sofa. It was a spur of the moment name, of no particular significance, though naturally he'd be delighted if his new friend turned out to be a descendent of Xie An, the calm, honorable statesman, or Xie Lingyun, the great landscape poet, both dating from the 4th or 5th century. Perhaps Xie Bomao was a descendant who just happened to be living in Nanjing today.

For the next few hours, Chen Yixin felt invigorated. He worked and chatted as normal, but every now and then he and Xie Bomao exchanged views, and somehow everything seemed bearable. Now and again, he thought about his daughter, and it made him smile, feeling as happy as she was.

At meetings during the day, at drinking sessions in the evening, and at night when he couldn't sleep, Chen Yixin got to know Xie Bomao a whole lot better. They were about the same age. Xie Bomao was troubled by a frozen shoulder. He liked unofficial histories and blue movies from Europe, because both made him feel alive. He was sick to death of conversations about online sensations, consumer price indexes, horoscopes, and things like that. He smoked, and he drank a bit. He didn't like it when people dressed in traditional Chinese garments on formal occasions, or used the word "brainstorm" at meetings.

Chen Yixin kept thinking about his daughter. Whenever she wanted more time on the computer, or another Ferrero Rocher, or wanted to wear her favorite sundress, she had a quiet discussion with Flying Fish, and then, with all seriousness, presented their shared point-of-view.

Then he thought about himself and shook his head with a knowing smile. No wonder Xie Bomao and he got on so well. Xie Bomao was practically his clone.

III

Li Fu had been to check place names at the local administration office so often that they were getting fed up with him. Each letter to Xie Bomao had a different address, most of which belonged to the days of yore. The locations had either been obsolete even before the Republic or had been flattened in recent decades to make wide new roads or vocational schools, government complexes, or Carrefour supermarkets. All of the old places had become new places.

Was there anything on Xie Bomao? The young woman in the registration office who never smiled did a search on the computer for Li Fu. There were four people with the name Xie Bomao in Nanjing. She saw the disappointment on his face, and shook her head at him.

"Well, can you tell me... does he have an online name, a Weibo account, or something? How about a class graduation photo? Any lead will do, something solid to flesh him out. You can find anyone if you can flesh them out a bit."

Li Fu didn't entirely understand what she meant, so reservedly expressed his gratitude and noted down the four addresses, which he planned to check out one by one.

The first Xie Bomao was away on business, and his wife — brandishing a stir-fry turner and in a resentful, acerbic tone of voice — insisted that he couldn't possibly have any friends, and slammed the door in his face.

The next Xie Bomao was the assistant manager of a famous sportswear store. He had a golden headset over his ears, and looked ready to engage in secret communication at any moment. He fingered the letter lightly and winked at the pretty sales assistant.

"Is this some kind of a joke?" he asked. But when he heard that Li Fu's son had just started working, he changed track, humoring him with attention and encouraging him to buy a pair of "the latest basketball shoes, launched simultaneously with the American market, limited edition, with built-in Bluetooth, calorie-counter, and air cushion," which he could let him have with a manager's discount of 22 per cent.

The third Xie Bomao was a primary school pupil with merit stripes on his shoulders. He was trudging across the playground, pulling a big book bag on wheels when he heard there was a letter for him. He slowed down, and though his face went red, he tried his best to maintain a serious composure. He glanced at his classmates nearby, and asked loudly, "From Yao Ming? Or Liu Xiang? I wrote to them both at the same time, and said I bet the other would reply first! But I sent them emails."

The last Xie Bomao was also the farthest away, in an industrial area north of the city. Li Fu made the long journey after work, when it was getting dark, and found him washing a Samoyed. As the hairdryer whirred around the dog, the man's worldly-wise tone of voice conveyed a hatred which he directed at Li Fu. "Well, aren't conmen getting clever! These days they even write letters! With a fucking calligraphy brush! Ingenious! Now, if you wouldn't mind ripping that up for me!"

Li Fu was worried, but there was no one he could talk to. His wife was always having a go at him for being "crazy." Forget his son, who was too embarrassed to tell anyone about his father's job. In this dog-eat-dog world, having a Model Worker for a father put him right at the bottom of the shit-heap, didn't it? He couldn't talk to his colleagues either. They were all so much younger than him and liked to talk about the UEFA Champions League, online games, and the quarterly bonus. If he told them about this Xie Bomao business, they'd flap their wings and fly away.

Li Fu decided to take a different approach. He'd put Xie Bomao to the side for the time being and look for Chen instead. He looked at the addresses again and again. He ran his fingers over them. The brush-written characters on the envelopes were easy on the eye, not too big, not too small. He tried to work out what was inside, maybe two or three sheets of paper. He held them up to the light, but the brown envelopes were too thick and he couldn't make anything out.

"Just open it and have a look!" his colleagues mocked as they walked past. Of course he could open it and see what was inside. He knew how to open a letter without leaving any evidence. He could open a letter and leave the postmark stamp over the seal perfectly intact. Obviously, it would not be a case of inappropriately "using one's position to destroy or conceal a letter" or anything like that. But, at the end of the day, a dead letter was still a letter, with all the dignity and regulations that a letter has. Opening it might provide a lead, but it would be tantamount to cheating, and that would be shameful, so he would not do it.

During his lunch break, Li Fu took his little green bag and cycled to the southern part of the city to look for stationery shops. There was one on Jinshajing Road, with lots of students inside, choosing all kinds of pens — erasable pens, highlighter pens, color-changing pens, scented pens, and so on — and there were lots of cute stickers, notebooks, and writing pads, which even he found attractive. There were girls picking up this and that, trying to decide which things to keep and which to put back. Li Fu drew a blank. He couldn't find what he was looking for, so he had to ask the salesperson, who directed him to the back of the shop, where, on the lowest shelf, he found envelopes and letter paper. There wasn't much of a choice, just one or two types, all very ordinary, and very ugly. But there was the exact same type of brown envelope that Chen used.

Li Fu realized how unpleasant and awkward it must be for Chen to have to crouch down in order to select these ugly envelopes. He crouched in that cold corner for a while, long enough for his legs to go numb, but didn't bump into another customer. That's right, he didn't "bump into" anyone. He'd been obsessed with finding a way to "bump into" Chen, and was still trying to think of places where that might happen.

He studied the postmarks on the letters. With one exception, they all were postmarked Zhonghuamen Post Office. On the postmark was a tiny serial number, indicating that the letters had been posted in the letterbox at the main entrance to the Post Office, or in the one in the Business Hall.

The next letter was imminent, so Li Fu spent several days hanging around the Zhonghuamen Post Office. He sat quietly at the desk in the Business Hall, watching people come and go. Or he stood across the road, staring at the tall letterbox at the entrance. Neither approach was effective. It could have been any, or none, of these people — you can't tell at a glance if a person writes letters with a calligraphy brush. And, in any case, hardly anyone posted letters in a letterbox nowadays. One day, he waited until half past five, and watched as the letterbox was opened and emptied of two pitiful letters. One was addressed to the Petition Office of the CPC Committee, the Government, the Political Consultative Conference and the People's Congress of Jiangsu Province, written with characters the size of broad beans, with two that were written incorrectly. The other envelope, which had not been sealed, had a wad of out-of-date lottery tickets stuffed inside it.

He sighed and thought about Chen, who took such care and was so persistent in writing to Xie Bomao about what could only be a very serious, very difficult matter. He would do his absolute best for this person. The more he thought about it, the less he liked the idea of "bumping into" Chen. The thought of having to return that pile of letters was just too sad.

IV

Chen Yixin's decision to pick up his brush and write to Xie Bomao had something to do with his daughter. Her kindergarten had recently been promoting the Montessori Method, encouraging our little friends not to study and practice, but to develop completely naturally, to the extent that today's homework required the parents to provide their child with paper, a brush, and twelve colors of paint, then let the child express him/herself. So that evening, they had covered the floor with newspaper, and his daughter and Flying Fish had spent ages painting. When she was tired, his wife went to put her to bed while he tidied up. He picked up a paintbrush, smoothed down the hairs, and started to write in indigo paint in the white space of the newspaper.

Chen Yixin had studied calligraphy during university, practicing the small, regular script with a fellow student for two and a half years. Afterwards, he'd been busy with his career and marriage, and it had fallen by the wayside. Writing a few characters now brought back some of those old feelings — yet they were not thoughts of university nor the springtime of youth, but of growing old and weak in the autumn of one's life. It felt very strange.

As he was throwing out the newspaper, he was shocked to discover what he had written. *Xie Bomao, Xie Bomao, Xie Bomao.* It seemed that he was thinking about his friend all the time, wherever he was, and that he had so much to tell him. After this shocking thought, he made a decision. He would tell him everything.

The next day, he went to buy envelopes and letter paper. They were of poor quality and not ideal, but they would do. After all, he'd seen too many things with a fine outward appearance that were rotten on the inside. During his lunch break, he lay back on the sofa, a bit restless and fidgety, as he thought about what he should write to Xie Bomao. He got up a few times, put his mobile on silent, changed his status on QQ to "invisible," turned off email and Weibo, and put the phone to one side. But none of this seemed to help. His mind was still a complete blank. He gripped the armrest of the sofa, scrunching up the real leather — perhaps he wouldn't be able to write anything? Maybe there were too many things on his mind to write? Or maybe there was nothing on his mind at all. Hmm, his daughter didn't seem to have this problem.

In the end, Chen Yixin accepted this state of uncertainty, took the couple of sheets of letter paper that he had prepared earlier, folded them carefully, and slipped them into the envelope. Never mind, he thought, Xie Bomao was his friend, and he'd "understand" what he had just "written."

He sealed the envelope, vaguely recalling the many different ways of folding letter paper. He could fold it into three vertically, then in half horizontally. Or he could fold it in half horizontally, then in half vertically. At school there'd been a classmate who could fold a piece of paper into a crane. He remembered all the business with postage stamps too. A stamp pasted upside down meant "I love you," two stamps side by side meant "I miss you," three stamps in a row meant "I'm waiting for your answer," and so on. There'd been a girl who liked to press her lips on the flap of the envelope to show it was sealed with a kiss. But he wasn't interested in things like that. They'd simply floated into his mind, remembrances of the past.

It was not until he came to write the address on the envelope that he felt the joy of ritual. Ah yes, a ritual! Nanjing had so many old place names that he liked, where the historical figures he liked had once walked. He closed his eyes and summoned up an old street or alley that had vanished long ago, and he let his satisfaction flow through brush and ink on to the envelope and into the obsolete address that would magnificently convey the entire content of the epistle.

The goat-hair brush in his hand was just about usable. It had been put aside for such a long time that insects had got to it. He could have bought a new one, but he liked its worn appearance, which matched his state of mind, with its loose ends and unspoken words. The letter writing soon became a habit, although there was no content in the letters, and the only writing was of one random old address after another as they came into his mind. The bald brush snagged and glided over the rough brown paper with no more noise than some lovely form of life landing softly and leaving its tiny traces on the world.

Afterwards, he went out and dropped the letter into the obviously empty letter box. In the hustle and bustle of the street, he pressed his ear to the opening and waited for the quiet echo, as though listening to a stone falling in a bottomless well. Down it fell, into the deepest place on earth, and continued its journey through this lonely spinning planet before reappearing and circling the moon, Saturn, and Jupiter, then entering space lit up by stars. Out there, somewhere, Xie Bomao was waiting for this letter. The process of letter writing was amazingly liberating for Chen Yixin, and it brought him enormous pleasure.

V

Li Fu had never forgotten a letter he'd seen in '87 or '88 that was written in traditional full-form characters on a traditional vertical-style envelope, sent from Hualian in Taiwan, to "Ms Zhang, of Qin (childhood name: Ziying)." On the back of the envelope was a message, written in a spidery hand, which said something like, "With heartfelt gratitude from an old soldier in Taiwan for your kind help in seeking my relative." But the address was old. It had long since been replaced with the Workers Cultural Palace, which itself had been closed for ages because there were plans to rebuild it as a fast food chain restaurant. The details were recorded in Li Fu's little notebook. The search had taken him a full five months, and it had been hard work. He had eventually found Ms Zhang at a hospice, thin as a loofah, with a constant dribble and afflicted with senile dementia. By her side was her droopy-eyed, sloppily dressed son in his forties, who opened the letter for her. He read a few lines, then suddenly started to shake.

"How could you lie to me?" he wailed. "It says here my father's still alive."

It was like a scene from a TV drama, and Li Fu sighed at the thought of it. Oh, these apparently ordinary human relationships — between husband and wife, between brothers, between father and son, between friends — were anything but ordinary. It was such a big, messy world. So much happens, and when it goes wrong, things fall apart. He wondered how Chen had lost contact with Xie Bomao. *Does Mr Xie know how hard you are trying to find him?* he wondered. *I really want to help you find him, you know.*

That evening, Li Fu had a dream, a pretty good one too. In his dream there was a loudspeaker, the kind that were standard in factories, mines, and production teams in the villages, and for some unknown reason, he heard his own voice being broadcast very loudly, with a buzz echoing in the background. *Attention. Attention. Will Comrade Xie Bomao make his way quickly to the post office. Will Comrade Xie Bomao...*

When he woke up, Li Fu thought he had the answer. If Xie Bomao didn't appear in the local residents' lists, then he must be from out of town. It all seemed to make sense. Li Fu felt re-invigorated. He could still hope to resolve these letters before he retired.

He spent time researching the place names presented as Xie Bomao's addresses. The Confucius Temple, the Prosecutor's Office, East of the Gate, and West of the Gate were all located in the southern part of the old city, so it looked as though that was Comrade Xie Bomao's haunt. A loudspeaker was out of the question, of course. But he always saw people at the bus or railway station holding up name boards to meet people, and salespeople by the roadside with placards advertising fridges and TVs. It was an idea — anyway, it was not something to be ashamed of. Li Fu made himself two cardboard placards, each a square of about 30 to 40 cm, wrote *Xie Bomao* with a black permanent marker on each one, made two small holes at the top corners, and threaded some string through the holes so the whole thing could hang over his shoulders like a vest. This way, the three large characters would be visible far away, from the front and the back.

Li Fu walked down Changle Road, Sanshan Street, Shuiguan Bridge, and Zhanyuan Road. He stuck out like a sore thumb, but either people were immune to the visual distractions around them, or they were no longer curious enough to bother asking. But he didn't lose heart. After all, if Xie Bomao hadn't been so hard to find, Chen wouldn't have written so many letters.

As he walked, he tried his best to imagine how someone here would live. Where he would go shopping, what he would buy, what he would eat, what he would see, what he would do for fun? Various thoughts came to mind – Home Inn, Giordano, SG, the 24-hour self-serve banking center, the snack bar selling duck blood soup with glass noodles, the subway entrance, the No. 1 Hospital, the Hai Di Lao Hotpot Restaurant, China Unicom 3G. When he thought of a place, he would go and take a look, all the time trying to stay within the southern part of the city. Every evening after work, he took advantage of the last hour or so of daylight to take a walk around. "Dripping water wears through rock" — this saying described him so well, he thought. As a child, he used to spend ages crouching under the eaves of the house, quietly watching the hollow in the stone as the drops of water fell.

Sometimes, his strings would get caught in the wind and his name cards would flip over. By the time he realized that the blank sides were showing, he'd have already walked down several streets. He thought about his wife, and how she called him crazy, and he couldn't help but laugh. Perhaps she was right.

He understood quite clearly that his search for Xie Bomao and his mission to rescue these dead letters were not the full story. There was some inexplicable pent-up sentiment that he felt, like a pain deep in his heart, that made him need to walk about with his little green bag over his shoulder, to keep wandering up and down and in and out of streets old and new.

VI

Chen Yixin was in the teahouse waiting for an old school friend who he hadn't seen in fifteen years. He'd been his best friend in the dorm for such a long time, and he was coming from out of town. But his flight was delayed, and Chen found himself killing time.

There was a blank memo pad on the table. Without thinking, he pulled it toward him and started doodling, just like the "Montessori teaching method" at his daughter's kindergarten. It was something he did to pass the time, during meetings, at lectures, waiting in line at the bank, waiting for planes, and so on. He didn't like playing on his cell phone, he couldn't stand those thick, heavy, strange-smelling magazines full of ads, and good old-fashioned reading seemed a bit pretentious these days.

All that waiting. Life was just a series of waiting, he thought. Waiting for people. Waiting for things. Waiting for contacts. Waiting for explanations. Waiting for things to start. Waiting for things to end. It might look as though waiting was subjective behavior, a democratic participation in and consultation with fate, when, in fact, all the endings were well, predetermined, or predestined. When the time comes, the results are quietly sitting there waiting for you. It's certainly never a question of you waiting for the results.

He doodled for a while until his friend turned up. They greeted each other enthusiastically, talked about the old days, ordered some food, and had a good sigh and a good moan, just shooting the breeze. They could carry on, or they could bring the conversation to an abrupt end. Either way, it didn't make much difference. As they both had to work that afternoon, they had arranged to hang out with some other guys that evening and have a good drink.

After his friend left, Chen Yixin sat for a while and felt the emptiness in his heart gape wider than before. This much anticipated meeting with his best friend from all those years ago had been a bit of a let down. Oh, never mind. He asked the waitress to bring the bill.

She had short hair and black-rimmed glasses. She gave him the print-out. "Lunch with 12% discount. Total 145 yuan. Are you paying cash or by card, Sir?" Chen Yixin gave her the once-over. The yellow scarf looked good with the dark waistcoat, and there was a green bowtie at her neck. He liked to look at restaurant uniforms, to see the different uniforms in their different settings, from the rustic local styles at the door to the fashionable Western style hosts in the karaoke lounge.

The waitress saw his smile, hesitated a little, then pointed to the memo pad at the corner of the table, and said, "Do you still need that, Sir? Xie Bomao…"

"Oh, it's nothing." Chen Yixin tore the note up and scrunched it into a ball. He hadn't realized what he had written. "That's my, er, a friend," he explained.

"Does he live round here then?" The way she asked was a little strange.

Chen Yixin nodded abstractedly as he took out his money. In his mind he was thinking that maybe in his next letter to Xie Bomao he'd "write" something about waiting.

"Well, I guess he must be the same person. Everyone here knows Xie Bomao. He walks down this road every evening," she said, pointing her chin towards the French windows. Chen Yixin's heart skipped a beat, as he slowly followed her line of vision. Outside, the leaves of the plane trees were falling to the ground, onto a scruffy newsstand, and onto those old bikes. He hadn't noticed that it was already the middle of autumn.

Chen Yixin made a quick calculation. He'd been writing letters to Xie Bomao for over a year now. He'd written about a passion that had been sealed in dust and buried in time, about a loved one so distant she might as well be dead. He'd written about a hushed scream. He'd written about ants — how people were like ants, and would climb here, there, and everywhere for a granule of sugar. He'd written about African animals mating in the wild — how the television masturbated silently at night.

Was it really possible that he had brought this Xie Bomao into being?

"How do you know he's Xie Bomao?"

"Well, he wears a placard on his chest, doesn't he? For months now, he's been coming and walking along this road at about six o'clock." She smiled. She had long slim fingers, and it was nice watching her clear the table. All afternoon Chen Yixin felt completely out of sorts. He seemed to see everything double, or as an illusion, distracted enough for one of the women at work to worry that he looked off. He struggled through to the end of the day, which was more or less the time the girl had said, then went round to the teahouse. He stood across the road, sort of waiting for a taxi. He was going to be drinking that evening, so he couldn't drive. While he was waiting, he bought a weekly at the newsstand.

When he looked up again, sure enough there was a *Xie Bomao* sign bobbing about in the crowd across the road. Three awkward looking characters on a filthy piece of cardboard, swinging on the back of an oldish man. Chen Yixin watched him the whole time, with eyes so wide they were almost popping out of their sockets. He could have called out to him, or gone after him, but for some reason, his legs felt heavy as lead, and worse, he felt shy and panicky. So he just stared with open eyes as "Xie Bomao" turned the corner into the next street.

He hurried as fast as he could to the bar in the western part of the city. His friend from out of town and the other guys had been hanging out there for a while. There were some women too — old school friends and family — quite a sight, and excited to be there.

Chen Yixin joined in the drinking, and it was all very lively. Later, they went to the karaoke lounge, where they sang and danced and carried on drinking until it was almost dawn, then they went their separate ways. When they stepped outside, they huddled

22

by the door, none of them quite in control of their hands and feet. Chen Yixin looked at them, and then at his own reflection in the glass wall. They were all equally a mess, a motley group of lonely souls and wild ghosts.

On the way home, Chen Yixin, breathing alcohol, slurred at the taxi driver, "Haha, I met an old friend today."

"Ah, an old friend, that's great," came the exhausted driver's perfunctory response as he wound down the window and turned up the radio.

Chen Yixin stretched his mouth and turned his burning face to the window. As the late autumn wind whooshed past, he could see a few faces hurrying along. He rested his hand softly on the window, and suddenly felt sad as he remembered the *Xie Bomao* cardboard sign, bobbing along on the other side of the road. It didn't matter if it was a man or a woman, human or ghost, or how stupid or thick it was, he might as well go and find it.

He thought about the stories he told his daughter every night before she went to sleep — so many fairy tales and myths, so many impossible yet beautiful things. But the Old Man up there only made fairy tales for children.

Chen Yixin didn't sleep at all that night. He thought about the bald brush and the stack of envelopes he hadn't finished. There was still half a bottle of Yidege liquid ink left. They were in his office, in the dark. The thought of not having any further use for them brought tears to his eyes. He was overwhelmed with dejection. The sudden appearance of this physical "being" meant that Xie Bomao's existence ceased to have any significance. He'd never be able to write another letter to this friend, who had been so difficult to find in the first place.

VII

Li Fu walked down the road to the teahouse wearing his *Xie Bomao* placard. Night was drawing in, and he was tired. *The end of another day*, he thought, and *nothing has changed*.

That morning, he had received his Model Worker Retirement Payment, which the union had awarded him in advance. It was a thick stack. His boss patted him on the shoulder and said, "After your honorable retirement, we plan to abolish the post of 'Dead Letter Rescuer.'"

Li Fu was in total agreement. "Good," he said. "It should be abolished. It's no use."

These last few days, as he'd walked up and down the streets, he'd seen people rushing along, yelling furiously into their mobiles, or crouching by the curb, furrowing their brows. The way they looked and moved filled him with disturbing associations. He thought about the evening paper he'd read, about the quirks of human relations that filled one with dismay, and pessimistically predicted that there'd be an irreparable regret — if these letters really were dead, they would be destroyed, pulped, and whatever the person called Chen had to say to Xie Bomao would be lost forever and ever. He wanted with all his heart to help.

He stopped at the corner of the road with the teahouse and thought about buying a bottle of water from the newsstand on the other side, but then decided not to. He'd rather his lips were dry. He had a strange way of looking at life, as though the harder it was, the more likely he was to reap rewards. In the past, when he'd chased up dead letters, he'd stumbled and fallen, sprained his foot, ripped his trousers, pushed his bike for miles with a flat tire — but in the end, he had rescued every single one of those dead letters.

The autumn wind stung his face. Winter was on its way. He'd walk round once more. After that, it'd get dark earlier each day, and there'd be even fewer people who noticed his *Xie Bomao* sign.

"Hey! Xie Bomao?" he heard someone call out to him. There was a question in the tone, an ordinary voice that was just audible.

Li Fu turned around, and saw a middle-aged man with no remarkable features behind his glasses. He was the fifth one. He'd been walking round for so many days, and this was only the fifth person to ask about Xie Bomao. As with the previous four, he had no intention of telling the whole story starting with the dead letters, lest the inquirer lose patience.

Li Fu beamed, held the placard straight and felt vindicated. It seemed he was right not to buy that bottle of water just now.

"Oh, I'm not Xie Bomao. I'm looking for him, for Xie Bomao. Are you... ?" he said.

"How long have you been looking for him?" It was getting dark, and the trees cast long shadows over his face.

Li Fu thought for a moment, and decided to start from the time of the first dead letter. "A year and two months."

The middle-aged man inched forward out of the shadows.

"Since last autumn?" His chin tilted upward. "And does he know you're looking for him?" The middle-aged man's face looked strained. His eyes skimmed over the grimy cardboard and then back to Li Fu's face.

"No. And he doesn't know me either." Li Fu knew this sounded ridiculous, and was anxious to keep it short, "Do you know him? This Xie Bomao?"

"No, I'm sorry, I don't know him. I was just asking." The middle-aged man nodded very politely and breathed out softly. Li Fu detected a sudden detachment that looked like sadness. *Maybe he thinks I'm mad*, he thought.

"The thing is, I'm helping someone who's looking for him." Li Fu saw the man was about to walk away, and was in two minds as to whether to tell him the whole story.

"Who are you helping, may I ask?" the middle-aged man halted, and something elusive began to flicker in his eyes again.

"Who am I helping? Well, I don't know that person either," said Li Fu, "but I know that this one's looking for that one, and maybe he's been looking for him longer than I have." He used his hands to demonstrate, nodding his head first to his left hand, then to his right, then back again.

The street lamps came on, and in the light, he could see that the middle-aged man had closed his eyes, as though he was closing something down inside. Then the man looked toward the road, and said very quietly, "You won't find him."

Well now, thought Li Fu, m*aybe this man really does know something about Xie Bomao.* He pushed the placard to one side and fumbled inside his green shoulder bag for his little notebook. He'd tucked the stack of money he'd received earlier inside the notebook, and he was trying to remove it without taking it out of the bag.

The middle-aged man looked at Li Fu's green shoulder bag, and stopped in his tracks. Suddenly everything fell into place. A faint mocking smile crept over his face, and without saying a word, he turned and walked away. It happened so fast that Li Fu didn't have time to say anything.

Li Fu's hand went still. He looked down at the green shoulder bag, and tried as hard as he could to work out what had gone wrong.

It would soon be completely dark. Li Fu looked around him, shook his head, and carefully removed the *Xie Bomao* sign. He looked at it for a while, then folded the white cardboard over and over into a small square, which took some effort, then struggled to shove it into a wastebin at the side of the road. *I'm sorry, Xie Bomao, I can't help you any more.*

Li Fu slowly headed home. Having taken off the *Xie Bomao* sign, he felt the icy northwest wind on his chest, but never mind, this was his last winter's day as the last Letter Rescuer. He felt the cash inside his green shoulder bag. He would try his best to be happy.

PARADISE
TEMPLE

Translated by **Brendan O'Kane**

I

Paradise Temple had none of the tranquility a graveyard ought to have in the early morning light. Two monstrous engines were roaring on a construction site just a few paces away, and the clanking, hammering construction workers had already gotten hot enough to strip down to their scarlet cotton knitwear. Fu Ma, meanwhile, was hunching against the cold. Da Guma, his father's sister, had wrapped a snake-print scarf around her neck. "These places are always colder than in the city," she muttered. Her husband was looking around in search of a toilet. Fu Ma fished out a pack of cigarettes, and Xiao Shushu, his father's younger brother, took one sleepily and leaned over to get a light from Fu Ma.

His paternal grandmother was the last one to get out of the car, supported by Xiao Guma, his father's other sister. A massive, old-fashioned gold ring glinted on Grandmother's hand, and she looked around appraisingly at the assembled family members before stepping out. All of them were wearing something gold —

to "weigh them down" in the graveyard — except for Xiao Shushu, who had forgotten and was left with no choice but to put a woman's braided gold necklace around his neck.

Grandmother usually knew enough, as an older person, to consult with the younger people in the family before going ahead with things, and to play dumb when necessary. When it came to visiting the graveyard, though, she was very particular. She would begin consulting the traditional calendar at the start of the lunar New Year, selecting an auspicious day and insisting that everyone, except for the children who were still in school, take a half-day off, the proceedings scarcely less lavish than a New Year's celebration. Not that it ever worked out exactly as she wanted — people were busy. This time, for instance, Fu Ma's father was out of the country, and Da Guma's daughter said she had an important job interview.

Grandmother looked around, wrinkling her brow. "What's this? Construction, even here?"

Her daughter-in-law — Fu Ma's mother — was talking into her phone about bed linens in careful newscaster Mandarin, haggling back and forth with the customer over some minor issue of price. The others listened, eyelids drooping, and Fu Ma stubbed out his cigarette. Finally, his mother laughed, curling her tongue. "We'll talk again, Mr Zhang — do keep me in mind the next time there's an opportunity."

Snapping her phone shut, she reverted to Nanjing dialect. "You hadn't heard? It was in the papers — they're moving the old Shizigang Crematorium to Paradise Temple. That's where the new building's going to go. How do you like that? Graves here are bound to get more expensive." In any situation that came up, her mind would go to what it would cost.

"Just as well," Grandmother said. "The old man always liked making friends. It'll be nice and lively here." She looked at the building site. The others looked too, their gazes hovering in mid-air as if the smokestack were already sticking up into the sky, with slow puffs of pale smoke rising from it.

By now the group had been surrounded by vendors proffering chrysanthemums, firecrackers, glutinous green rice balls, paper mansions, cardboard sedans, and the like. The family members knew enough to ignore these and walk straight ahead.

Grandmother had already taken care of planning the grave-offerings. She had set aside stacks of gold and silver grave-money at home a month in advance and phoned everyone to tell them what to bring – red silk ribbons, bananas (she specified Chinese-grown plantains), red Fuji apples, Nanking cigarettes (the ones in golden packs), Yanghe liquor, candlesticks, incense — sounding a little like a public service worker as she reminded them that everyone would have to do their part and bring something small, even just a lighter.

Xiao Shushu lingered behind the group. Unable to resist the vendors, he bought a willow twig, then ran forward, his shoulders slumping, to join the others. He had been taking part in less and less family events since the divorce. The previous year, he'd brought a big-breasted girl he was dating along to the Midautumn Festival dinner, but for the grave visit, he was alone again.

The path into the graveyard took them past a long flight of steps. Da Guma and her younger sister, who were usually arguing with each other about something or other, now walked hand in hand, looking around and quietly discussing the gravestones along the way. *This is a new grave, from a burial just before the lunar New*

Year. That one has three people in it. Would you look at that picture, how bright that young man looks? Such a pity.

As they approached Grandfather's grave, Grandmother was drawn first to the two young cypress trees that flanked it, just like every other year, and she clasped her hands in front of her as she addressed her descendants. "See? Still growing — and so green! The old man down there is looking after you all."

Her sons and daughters nodded hurriedly, as if receiving signals from Grandfather via the trees, and their responses were more or less the same as they were every year. "Yes, yes, Dad is looking after us."

Two shabbily dressed strangers approached, a man and a woman, and Fu Ma was startled to see the man begin clicking a pair of wooden clappers he held in his hand. "Wealth and riches, sir! Wealth and riches, ma'am! Wealth and riches, mister! Wealth and riches, miss! Wealth and riches for the whole family! Wealth and riches for many generations to come!" At every pause, the woman beside him barked out a rhythmic "Yes!"

The two drew closer, chanting their rough benediction. Xiao Guma's husband reached into his pocket for money, but Da Guma's husband raised a hand to stop him. "Let them keep going for a while longer. Very good."

The noise from the construction site quieted suddenly, and the surrounding gravestones pricked up their ears and held their breath, listening to the man and woman chanting in their Huaibei accent, "Wealth and riches, sir! Yes! Wealth and riches, ma'am! Yes! Wealth and riches, mister! Yes! Wealth and riches, miss! Yes! Wealth and riches for the whole family! Yes! Wealth and riches for many generations to come! Yes!"

Fu Ma patted his cigarettes, but stifled the urge to take one. He had long discovered that those who claimed to have no patience for superstition, no matter how domineering or willful they usually were, always ended up going along with things once they got here, proceeding dreamily but earnestly with every step of the complicated process – brushing away the dust from the grave and tying the red ribbons around it, then offering incense, lighting cigarettes, raising toasts of liquor, kneeling and touching their foreheads to the ground before the grave, setting the paper money alight and calling out with affection one after another for Grandfather to accept it, and so on and so forth, including listening to the chant now.

Pleased, almost greedily, Fu Ma took in the sight of his assembled relatives. None of them looked anything like their usual card-playing, eating-and-drinking, squabbling, familiar selves, including him. Every year, Fu Ma took his time when he knelt before the grave, as if savoring the rare ritual – how the knees bent, how the buttocks lifted, how the head inclined deeply toward the concrete, his eyes taking in the shoes next to him and the rough earth as it approached. It seemed as if his forehead would hit the ground in an instant, and also as if it would never hit the ground.

And now — there was another important matter to be discussed, the writing on the tombstone.

It had been eight years, after all, and the characters on Grandfather's tombstone had faded, the black characters to gray, the red characters to white. It didn't look good. Next to some of the new tombstones nearby, or the tombstones whose characters had been redone, Grandfather's tombstone looked neglected, as if it had been abandoned to the elements.

Redoing the characters would be easy enough. The graveyard would take care of it for them, for a fee. The problem was, there had been changes in the family over the past eight years, and one or two of those changes involved family members whose names were inscribed in red on the tombstone. Next to Xiao Shushu's name, for instance, was the wife he had divorced. Xiao Guma's son had changed his name the previous year, after a fortuneteller told him he needed more of the "water" element in the written characters to balance out his luck.

"And then there's Fu Ma," Xiao Guma's husband murmured to Fu Ma's mother.

"You said he'll be getting married at the end of the year? If we're going to redo the tombstone, we'll want to add the name of the old man's granddaughter-in-law."

Fu Ma had been distracted, but at the mention of his name he quickly waved a hand in an attempt to decline, as if he were turning down a drink at a banquet or yielding the floor in a meeting, then thought better of it. His throat tightened with a sudden fear. Getting married? Really? Then stuck together for the rest of their lives — it was hard for him to imagine. And anyway, he was pretty sure she wouldn't like the idea of carving her name onto a tombstone in Paradise Temple that belonged to an old soldier from Shandong whom she'd never met, who had crossed the Yangtze and liberated Nanjing and with whom she would have had nothing at all to talk about. She barely even spoke to Fu Ma these days. The inexplicable chill had begun right about the moment they had set the wedding date.

Pulling rank as the wife of the eldest son, Fu Ma's mother observed the angle of Grandmother's raised eyebrows for a few seconds before saying, "If that's how we're going to do things, who knows how many times we'll have to change the tombstone? What if Fu Ma's Xiao Shushu remarries? Or if Fu Ma and the other children have children of their own?"

Grandmother shook her head at the tombstone as if Grandfather were sitting there. "You see how it's been," she sighed. "So many problems in the family that you haven't even heard about."

Fu Ma had a guilty sense that she was talking about him. He hadn't done a damn thing with himself these past years but fallen in and out of love with a succession of questionable girlfriends who had been judged by his family and found wanting. The oldest had been 12 years his senior, while two were girls from other cities he'd met online. One had burst into his house holding a sonogram and tried to slit her wrists. Another had actually started flirting outright with Xiao Shushu. He looked up, guiltily, and was startled to see that everyone present wore an embarrassed expression. True enough, they had all had their share of problems. Da Guma's husband, who worked as an overseer of construction projects, had narrowly escaped a corruption probe, and Xiao Guma had embarked upon a thrilling and ill-advised extramarital relationship. And Mother had been tricked into investing everything in a pyramid scheme, even Grandmother's retirement money.

Da Guma's husband shifted his weight back and forth — he had to pee again. Xiao Guma rubbed her nose red with a tissue before piping up, "If you ask me, I think we should go by what was on the tombstone to begin with. That was what Dad knew about, and we should keep to that."

It was a reasonable thing to say. Faces relaxed and everyone looked over at the tombstone, as if the dates carved into it eight years earlier had assumed a new meaning. The pale grey incised characters were written in a stiff, thick Wei-style script, and the family members' gazes played over them unhappily. Eight years was a long way to look, too long by far to make out clearly. They all bid farewell to Grandfather before leaving the graveyard. This was Grandmother's rule, too. They only came once a year, so why not say something to the old man?

The sun rose through the slightly grubby fog, shining down on the vast, crowded graveyard, down on the tomb slabs that lay flat on the ground, down on the tombstones covered with names of ancestors, deceased, and descendants, down on the old green cypress trees that stood between the tombs and the gravestones, and on their little group. Fu Ma's mother and aunts had made themselves up carefully and dressed for the occasion, Fu Ma noticed, but they and the men looked old, saggy, weak, and powerless here in the sunlight.

Mom closed her eyes, her unevenly mascaraed eyelashes fluttering. "Your oldest son is out of the country again, Dad. You know I don't like it when he flies, so make sure you take good care of him and see that he gets there safely. And look after all the rest of us. And look after my business — you know how it is. I still have to pay back Mother's money." She nattered on and on, as if she were chatting at the family dinner table. Fu Ma poked her.

Da Guma's husband cleared his throat. "Yingying, who you always liked so much — she's going to be starting work this year, so you don't have to worry about her."

Da Guma stepped forward and added, quietly, "I know you'll look after Yingying, Dad. Her interview today is really important. A foreign company, so it's all in English."

"Good health, that's what matters most," Xiao Guma's husband said, pressing his palms together. "Your grandson's a bright boy, so when he takes his exams for the Foreign Languages School next year, just make sure he can perform like he always does." He spoke as if emphasizing the simplicity of his desires, as if he didn't dare trouble the old man by asking for too much.

"I went around to a lot of different stalls today, Dad, but they only had imported bananas," Xiao Guma said. "I don't know why, but I had to look all over to find plantains for you, and when I finally found a place that had them, the seller called me 'ma'am,' like I was an old woman."

Fu Ma nearly laughed at this, but noticed suddenly that Xiao Guma was crying. Her husband's face was blank and unmoving. The two had been living apart for some time now, ever since her affair had started. Fu Ma remembered when the two of them were still in love. They'd take him to the zoo, then leave him to fend for himself while they snuck off behind the giraffe pens to kiss each other. He could almost see it now.

Xiao Shushu dragged his feet. He asked Fu Ma for a cigarette and took a few drags before setting it upright on the gravestone. His lips moved faintly, as if he were whispering to Grandfather, but nobody could hear what he was saying, including Grandfather, who had been so deaf the two years before his passing that lightning could have struck right next to him without him noticing.

Now it was his turn, and as in previous years Fu Ma found himself at a loss for words. He had never gotten used to the ceremony — as if Grandfather had stopped being Grandfather after he died and started being a Bodhisattva to whom they could entrust their health, professional careers, and grades at school. Fu Ma's mother, standing off to one side, finally lost patience and spoke up to offer a prayer on his behalf. "You see? Hopeless. Take care of his marriage, please, for our sakes."

Grandmother lingered behind to stand on her own at the grave for a few minutes. As she got back into the car her expression was unreadable, but peaceful. It was only 11:00, but they went for lunch together at the usual restaurant. Da Guma's husband could pick up the check here, and the state would foot the bill.

Yingying joined them, fresh from her interview. Despite the cold, she was wearing only a cream-colored suit, her waist almost invisibly narrow, and a pair of stilt-like leather shoes. The others looked like squat, bloated hens in comparison as they surrounded her and pressed her for details about the interview, and she answered easily, occasionally sprinkling her responses with English. As a member of the third generation, Yingying always became the center of attention at family gatherings. One of the viaduct projects her father oversaw had covered three years at an Australian college Fu Ma could never remember the name of, rendering the "Education" section of her CV instantly a million times prettier than his own, and now it looked as if her "Previous Employment" section would follow suit. What was Fu Ma, anyway, never mind Yingying. Pick any ten people off the street and eight of them would be better than him, or so his mother said, and he agreed. Yingying greeted him warmly and complimented him on his "stylish shirt." He looked down and saw he was still wearing his jacket, with only a small corner of his shirt peeking out.

Xiao Guma had gone to pick up her son Doudou from school. "The food at that school is no better than pigswill," she said.

Fu Ma barely recognized the little butterball who panted as he called out, "Hi, big brother!" — when had Doudou put on the extra weight? He looked like one of the fat kids in American movies who was always getting pushed around. Doudou carried a little book with him, and at his mother's prompting he sat down in a corner to study, his lips moving silently as he read. Fu Ma went over to another corner to get a cigarette, not wanting to bother him. After five or six minutes, he realized Doudou wasn't turning the pages of his book at all. Aside from his lips, which moved almost imperceptibly, the boy looked just like a statue. Fu Ma thought back sadly to a memory of Doudou from a meal like this one a few years before. The boy had been chirpy as a magpie, with an enviable memory that let him rattle off pitch-perfect imitations of TV commercials word for word. "Grandma's cooking is blah. Moooooooom! Use Taitaile bouillon cubes! Tasty and fresh, just like it should be!"

"Time just keeps ticking away. There are 24 hours in the day — how many do you save for yourself? Stop, treat yourself, and baby your beauty with Meiji facial masks."

"The all-new Chery Cowin. Save money. Save gas. Sturdy safety with style."

The family members pulled out chairs for each other, all of them insisting on being the last one to sit down. Grandmother took the seat of honor and directed Yingying and Doudou to sit on either side, as if in recognition of their roles as future captains of industry. Fu Ma's mother shot him a surreptitious look, a complicated expression flashing across her face despite her best efforts to hide it. Fu Ma hated that about her. So they were successful, he thought — so what? Next to him sat the perpetually morose Xiao Shushu, who patted his shoulder sympathetically in a way he probably thought was comforting. Grandmother was still talking to Da Guma. "Oh, Yingying should have called and told us so we could tell the old man the good news back at Paradise Temple! Hired on the spot — amazing!"

Fu Ma picked up his chopsticks. He was hungry, not having had time for breakfast, but didn't know where to begin. Grandmother had picked the dishes – braised tofu with greens, sweet potato noodles, ribbonfish, bean sprouts. All of these were mandatory after a visit to Grandfather's grave. The others were things Grandfather had always liked — red-braised eel, sweet steamed pork with brined cabbage, salted fish, dried stinking tofu with artemisia, stinky tofu, scallion buns. The family members spun the Lazy Susan that held the dishes, turning their attention to the task of eating on Grandfather's behalf.

Once they had lifted their chopsticks, nobody said another word about Grandfather. They reverted to their usual topics of conversation, just like at New Year's and Midautumn Festival, playing the same old allotted roles, spouting the same moldy old lines.

Da Guma's husband was unabashed in discussing the source of his pain, his swollen prostate. "It just keeps getting worse," he said, looking around the table at the others as he ate. "I had to go four times at the graveyard just now. I don't know how they haven't got a cure yet. It affects as many as half the people in the damned world."

Xiao Guma's husband was talking to Xiao Shushu about cars. "Most things you can't trade up on," he guffawed. "People, say. May as well trade up on cars." He glanced at Xiao Guma as he spoke. Xiao Shushu responded with an analysis of different cars' fuel usage, and the two men were transported back by memories of the oil prices of three years, four years, even five years before, a series of low and insignificant figures.

Xiao Guma discussed a writing assignment with Doudou, carefully picking bones out of his fish as if the boy were a three-year-old.

Da Guma and Fu Ma's mother were discussing the endocrine system and liver spots, rejuvenating poultices, uterine tumors, and the timing of menopause, their voices sharp as only middle-aged women's could be. Yingying sipped her soup daintily as she listened, occasionally chiming in to offer the latest international findings, such as that the best way to ensure ovarian health was to lead a regular sex life, especially after menopause. Turning his attention to a crumbling piece of stinky tofu, Fu Ma thought of the times his girlfriend had argued with him about contraception over the phone, wondering to himself if this was what all women were like now. But he remembered the girls he'd seen when he was younger, their clean, shy beauty, and how he had fallen in love with them.

Ah, the girls of yesteryear. There were no real girls in the world anymore, he thought. There was nothing left, nothing but boredom, sky-darkening, suffocating boredom.

With nothing else to do, Fu Ma lowered his head and began playing with his phone. His mother glared at him from across the table, and he was sure she would have kicked him if her legs were long enough. *You think I want to be playing with my phone, Mom? You think all those people playing with their phones while they cross the street or sit on the toilet want to be playing with their phones? What else am I supposed to do, when everything is so pointless and boring?*

He'd switched to a new phone just recently, and he tapped his way aimlessly through its menus until he found a World Clock. Global Weather Forecast. Pedometer. Calorie Counter. Flashlight. Bar Dice. Kingsoft PowerWord (English and Japanese). Panorama Editor. He tried out each of these. It passed the time, anyway. Especially Stopwatch. He watched the numbers flipping past on the screen — 10, 50, 80 — so fast he couldn't keep track — 100, and there, one second had passed. The numbers blurred together again — another second. He watched, genuinely rapt.

Xiao Shushu nudged him, and Fu Ma looked up to see Grandmother conveying a chopstick-load of sweet-braised pork toward his plate, as if to console him for having been left on his own. He rose, quickly, and held his bowl out to receive it. "Eat well while you're still young," she mumbled. "The more, the better." All the authority had left her expression, Fu Ma noticed. Now that the visit to Grandfather's tomb was finished, she had gone back to being an afterthought, a bystander. She sat down unsteadily, two bean sprouts stuck to the front of her shirt, working half a scallion bun with her remaining teeth. Fu Ma watched her for a moment with a faint, newfound sense of respect. He felt very full all of the sudden.

Da Guma's husband's phone rang, and he answered in a tone that made it clear this was an important call. The others fell silent, remembering that he was the one paying for this meal. Da Guma waved over a waitress with an exaggerated gesture. Xiao Guma quietly asked Doudou if he'd like one more piece of pork. Yingying took out a compact and freshened up her lipstick. Xiao Shushu stuck a hand into Fu Ma's coat, fishing for cigarettes, and as if in thanks leaned forward and whispered clearly, suddenly emotional,

"A word of advice — you're better off not getting married. Really. I've spent a lot of time thinking about it, and — well, you've seen it too. There's not much of a point, really."

Fu Ma looked up sharply, but Xiao Shushu closed his eyes and exhaled a big puff of smoke into the air above the table.

Chairs scraped against the floor, squeaking unpleasantly, making their movements as they stood, donned coats, and tied scarves even more reminiscent of animals scattering. Grandmother leaned against the table as she rose to her feet, looking wistfully at the remaining food as she grumbled about the waste — nobody taking a doggy bag, not even to feed the neighborhood strays. No one paid any attention. The waitress returned with the check, but Da Guma's husband had run off to the bathroom again, and so they all stood there patiently, nobody even making the pretense of trying to pay.

Something occurred to Grandmother as she looked around, and she pulled Da Guma toward her solemnly, then, after thinking a moment, did the same with Fu Ma's mother. "After I'm gone, it'll be up to you two to take care of all this. Plan it in advance, and don't forget to check the old calendar to find an auspicious day!"

"What are you talking like that for?" Da Guma asked, shaking her head. "You're still in fine shape." She pursed her lips as she tied her scarf in a bow.

Fu Ma's mother made a fuss over Da Guma's new scarf, but quieted after she found out what it had cost, her interest considerably lessened. She turned toward Grandmother, repeating Da Guma's words. "You're in great shape."

Grandmother carried on briskly while she still had their attention, "You two remember what foods I like, don't you? Besides the old man's favorites, you'll have to remember to order rice porridge, soup dumplings, snails stir-fried with chives, and osmanthus pudding with red beans." These were dishes from Changzhou, where Grandmother was from.

Fu Ma grabbed his phone as he got up. The stopwatch was still running, and he hit the "Stop" button: 00:21:37:95. He stared for a moment before realizing that this was the 21 minutes and 37.95 seconds that had passed just now, right here, in this room.

He snickered.

Xiao Shushu stubbed out his cigarette. "What are you sneering at?" he asked, a little touchily.

II

Fu Ma stood at the side of the road, his arm raised. A taxi pulled up, but the driver got out and flopped a hand in Fu Ma's direction ambiguously before walking to a sidewalk newspaper kiosk to buy two packs of yellow paper and a few bundles of ghost money. He lit a cigarette as he got back into the car, and began talking away at Fu Ma as if he'd known him for years. "Look it, the money's got pictures of foreigners all over it. Is that Washington or Clinton? Bet my mother never thought I'd be burning American dollars for her."

Fu Ma nodded in response, thinking meanwhile that it would be a waste to go back to the office so early. He didn't have to clock in until 2:30, and even a little later would be fine, since everyone knew he had been to visit his grandfather's grave. Might as well do something. Though he'd have to arrange it first.

Fortunately, "the girl" was logged into QQ Chat day and night. That was her screen name, "The Girl." Fu Ma had met her through QQ's "message in a bottle" feature, which let users send messages to other random users nearby. Some of the ways people used the feature were indecent, but honest in their indecency, and you could quickly look through the crowd to find people who were looking for the same thing. "The Girl" was two years older than Fu Ma, and he thought she had marriage plans of her own. They didn't do much talking when they met — there was no pretense of romance or tenderness. It sounded cold, when you put it that way, but whatever — you couldn't be too picky with this sort of thing. The weirder the better, in some ways.

"The Girl" cheerfully accepted his suggestion. She said she'd just been sitting around anyway.

By then the cab was nearly at Fu Ma's office, and he had to tell the cab driver to turn around and head for the other side of town. The driver chuckled knowingly upon hearing that the destination was the Hanting Express motel and made a big show of sighing and furrowing his brow. "Ooh, that's a ways away. Might take a while, so cool your jets."

He turned on the radio and sat back in his seat as if preparing for a long haul. After the grating stock reports and grating commercials, a more grating announcer came on and launched into a seasonal report about natural burials, tree burials, burials at sea, flower-bed burials, all in the same tone of voice you'd use to talk about regional cuisines, then attempted to be clever by posing the question to his listeners of whether they'd rather be buried under a bed of peonies or a clutch of rosebushes, and whether they would prefer a burial at sea in the Pacific Ocean, the Arctic Ocean, or

Mochou Lake downtown. He even started talking about how some small city overseas had come up with an environmentally friendly design that had the city's crematorium providing free heating for the city's bakeries. Fu Ma nearly choked on his own spit at the thought of bread baked using human bodies for fuel.

The traffic grew heavier, and soon the taxi was locked in bumper-to-bumper traffic in an underground tunnel. A line of sickly pale fluorescent lights hung overhead like a paper necklace, making it feel like the depth of night. The cab driver flicked irritably through the channels, but got nothing but static. His breathing grew labored, as if there were floodwaters rising to his neck. "I hate tunnels," he said. "All of them — the Xuanwu Lake Tunnel, the Jiuhua Shan Tunnel, the Fugui Shan Tunnel, the Yangtze River Tunnel – all of them. Now they're saying they're going to tear down the Hexi Overpass and put in a tunnel there too. I won't be able to work if they keep doing it, I'm telling you."

Fu Ma passed him a cigarette, which he took reluctantly, rolling his eyes. "I didn't used to be like this, but after the Wenchuan quake I just lost my nerve. I can't even ride the subway anymore, you couldn't get me on there for anything. How about you? You don't worry there'll be an earthquake or something?"

Fu Ma nearly laughed at the brusque tone the driver had affected while saying these things, but he was too busy calming down "The Girl" on QQ, explaining to her that he'd be late.

"There's a thick air of Hades about Nanjing, don't you think?" The cab driver was still going. "Whenever people from out of town get into my car, they always want to go to the same places — the Xiaoling Mausoleum, or Sun Yat-sen's Mausoleum, or Yuhuatai Revolutionary Martyrs Memorial Park, or the Nanjing Massacre

Memorial, or the Taiping Rebellion Museum, or the Southern Tang Tombs. Even the old Presidential Palace or the Qinhuai River. It's the same thing, isn't it? 'Ancient city' this and 'capital of six dynasties' that, just layer after layer of dead people, stacked on top of one another."

Fu Ma nodded absentmindedly. He was more absorbed in planning the afternoon's positions with "The Girl." Plans would change once they actually got down to it, but you could call it a kind of foreplay. Time was tight, after all.

The cars ahead finally began to move, and the cab driver instantly started twiddling the radio dial again, flooding the car with noise. He seemed a little bit annoyed at Fu Ma's coldness. "Aw, look at you. Like you're really that busy." After a moment, he continued, to himself, "Nothing wrong with it. Get it while the getting's good."

Fu Ma glanced up at the driver. Sometimes he just wasn't in the mood to speak. He might have chatted if the driver had been on QQ too.

Finally they rose above the ground, and Fu Ma turned his gaze to the bleak streets outside. He tried framing the view with four fingers, as if this would make it more pleasant. As he looked through the little rectangle, he noticed for the first time that many of the cigarette shops, convenience stores, and newspaper kiosks were displaying paper grave-money and tinfoil gold bricks alongside the newspapers, chewing gum, and bottled water, like a special hand signal, a patiently repeated code sign flashing at the pedestrians hurrying past. Fu Ma was startled. The cab driver sensed an opportunity to regale him. "They sell that stuff all the time — the Ghost Festival, the winter solstice, New Year's Eve, the Qingming Festival, it's all over the place. You see people burning it too, when it comes to someone's death anniversary or birthday. You young people, just thinking about your own pleasure — you might have forgotten, but everyone dies sooner or later."

Fu Ma parted his lips, lowered his phone, and turned back to stare through the window at the paper money as they fluttered in the breeze, fell into the distance behind them, reappeared, and vanished again. Fragments of the driver's chatter played intermittently in his brain, as if on a tape delay. Grabbing the seat to keep from swaying as the car turned, he was struck by a sudden sense that this car was the very last one in the city, that it was rushing toward an apocalyptic date through a crowded yet desolate land where the bodies of the dead and the ruined splendors of the past were lurching back to life from where they lay, one on top of another, sighing deafeningly.

After showering, they always enjoyed lying in bed and chatting for a while. "The Girl" complained that her new pair of Belles was hurting her feet, then got onto the subject of a body composition analysis she had done at the gym recently – her PBF, her SMM, her WHR. Her body was something she cared about deeply, and left to her own devices, she might have been able to talk about the topic for hours, even if Fu Ma never said a single word. One time she discussed the history of her hair, starting four years earlier – hair extensions one Valentine's Day, a bob cut one birthday, this color that summer vacation, that softening product the other weekend, all recounted in meticulous detail. It made Fu Ma feel sad, the utter solidity of his loneliness.

As she continued her constant autobiography, Fu Ma turned on the television and flipped through the channels until he found Animal Planet. It was the same thing as always — scenes of stalking and strategizing, leopards and hyenas and their long-running disputes about the allocation of both fresh and old meat — but Fu Ma thought it would work well enough as background noise. He watched the screen out of the corner of one eye as he began to caress "The Girl" and her PBF, her SMM, her WHR. "The Girl" squirmed and started complaining about her migraines, how her head had been hurting for almost a week now, not badly, true, but constantly – not enough to affect anything, but certainly not comfortable at any rate, sometimes on the left, but then the next day at the back of her head.

Fu Ma kept busy, hoping to improve her mood, and hoping to improve his own too. For a few moments, then, he felt as if time had slowed down, softly congealing like candle wax, and a despondent feeling wrapped itself tightly around him. He could hardly recognize himself at that instant — an instant too tedious to be of note, spent on a bed he would never use again, with a girl who talked absentmindedly the whole time. He looked almost pleadingly at the television, where a hyena, his moment come, was now tearing greedy mouthfuls from a putrid gazelle carcass against a tangerine sunset, his muzzle flecked with bloody spatters of meat.

Turning the other direction, Fu Ma looked at his phone next to the pillow — a small, finely made square of metal for which, in this helpless moment, he felt a sudden teary warmth welling up in him like a geyser. If nothing else, it was the one thing in the world with which he was truly intimate, the only thing that retained his body temperature and his scent. It was like an all-purpose shim that could fill in every ugly, impassable gap in his life. This one, for instance. An idea came to him. He could use the Timer function to see how long the encounter would take. Might be fun, anyway! But he just couldn't work up any enthusiasm, no matter how he tried, and he felt his hands growing sweaty on the girl's body. Perhaps he had been too hasty today — especially after the meal, with all those depressing little details piling up and all his relatives and himself even more disappointing than usual. It was like reminding him of every unhappy aspect of his life at once. And then there was that chickenshit cab driver and all his talking.

"The Girl" jerked and clapped a hand to her mouth. "Oh, I know! The migraine — it must be my dad thinking of me. I was thinking, it's almost time for the Tomb Sweeping Festival, and every year this time there's always something uncomfortable happening — a fever, or problems with my stomach, or my skin starts itching, and medicine and drips won't take care of it – but as soon as I go visit my father and burn some paper for him, everything clears up right away. Really, for the past few years — it's amazing! Tomorrow, tomorrow I'll go."

Fu Ma was startled, not at what she was saying but at how his body reacted — it was as if a violent rush of hormones took over and forced him to jump on top of her, like a robot whose "on" button had been pushed. "The Girl" grunted, then began to emit long, thin moans of pleasure.

Fu Ma hadn't forgotten to press the Start button on his phone, and he watched out of the corner of his eye as the numbers on the timer began to roll by. Frozen time, slapped back to life, began churning in his body and hers, rushing, zooming faster and faster. He held his breath, as if he were riding a dangerous horse, and as his nerve endings grew engorged he smelled the gamy reek of decay and corruption, and imagined himself as the hyena wolfing down his dinner in the weeds. But another program had come on the television, an Unsolved Mysteries sort of thing. The host was staring out at Fu Ma's contorted posture with an inscrutable expression. Pouting at the announcer, Fu Ma pointed at the timer on his phone, at the churning numbers, in hopes of distracting himself and prolonging this instant that seemed the only remaining proof of his ability to feel. The wind whistled in his ears. A bestial panting came from beneath him. He clenched his teeth and prepared to fight, to shake off, break away from the figure that forever dogged his footsteps, face half-concealed, black robe fluttering, casting the long thin shadow of Death.

There was a sudden, loud sob from "The Girl" and tears began running down her face and onto the pillow. She dug her fingers into Fu Ma's back and said, falteringly, "You — my — my headache's gone."

Everything around him was as dark and calm as the depths of the ocean. He could almost see the undulating fronds of seaweed and the deep blue light shining down from above. He had become a single transparent cell, expanding constantly in all directions.

Fu Ma opened his eyes slowly, saw the crappy light fixture hanging from the ceiling, the art print on the wall, the lifeless, limp window drapes, and the dim light beyond them that signaled the onset of dusk. It had been a long, deep sleep, as if he had been transported to another world. If only he could have stayed there.

Fu Ma wriggled his legs and arms. No wonder he was tired, given how early he'd had to wake up this morning to go to Paradise Temple. He glanced at the time – too late now even to clock out of work. Not a problem. He could try asking a coworker to run the fake rubber fingerprint he'd bought online over the scanner.

He tapped out a text message blearily, dreading the sensation of warmth returning to his body as if from some distant plane, and with it the capacity to perceive grief and happiness. Despair — at having nothing to his name, nowhere to turn to — began rumbling afresh, like a freight train right on schedule, soon to crush him beneath its wheels. This was no surprise. It happened every time after sex. It was his brain's revenge on his lower body for leaving it alone with its own wretchedness, a complication no medicine could treat.

He showered and dressed, gazing at his slightly distorted reflection in the mirror and noting that his stubble had darkened. His mother had remarked on this at Paradise Temple this morning, though it sounded like she was complaining about the price of the electric razor. At 680 kuai a pop, you had to shave every day for it to be worth it. But stubble was one of the body's crops. Why shave it all off? Embarrassment? So what if he didn't want to shave? Would his coworkers or his bosses be looking at him closely enough to notice? He didn't look at them closely, either. Fair was fair.

The clerk downstairs looked preoccupied as Fu Ma paid, as though she too had her fair share of worries, and she regarded him with a sympathetic expression. Or maybe he was looking at himself through her eyes. Annoyed, Fu Ma looked straight at her, rudely, until she lowered her gaze. He looked around. Seeing a *No Smoking* sign, he took out a cigarette and lit it, feeling a little more cheerful now.

At that instant, Fu Ma thought of Grandfather. At that instant, an instant he'd been planning to forget, to squander — the instant he accepted his wrinkled change from the clerk — he remembered his dead grandfather.

There was a time, early on weekend mornings, as early as he'd left for Paradise Temple this morning, when Grandfather would take young Fu Ma, not yet a teenager, to the outskirts of the city to climb the Purple Mountain. They'd start from White Horse Park, on a path that began on a gentle grade before growing steeper, passing pack after pack of panting hikers, sometimes with white puppies or big golden dogs, and people listening to rousing old songs on hand-held radios. On the right-hand side of the path walked people focused on climbing the mountain. On the left-hand side, more relaxed crowds descended contentedly, the two sides complementing each other like a self-contained circulatory system. There was a pleasantness about the mountain path that seemed completely independent from the world below. Sometimes, Grandfather would pause for a moment at a kiosk, counting out his wrinkled small change to buy a cucumber and a tea egg for Fu Ma. A moment later, he would take Fu Ma's hand and they would slip back into the crowd, tiredly but assuredly continuing their slow climb toward the observation deck at the mountain's verdant summit. Fu Ma's legs trembled, as if that vanished, impossible happiness were slapping against his calves.

He glanced up at the clerk one last time, embarrassed at the tears in his eyes, and saw no surprise in her expression. Twenty-five minutes later, Fu Ma stood at the foot of the Purple Mountain, on the path that started from White Horse Park. The place had changed, but he still felt a vague sense of familiarity. He was surprised at the number of people walking on the path in couples and groups, some of them talking and laughing, a vision of the everyday. Who'd have thought there'd be so many people climbing Purple Mountain at night? He couldn't make out any of their faces, though these weren't the same people as before, that was for sure.

The night was like a thick, heavy gown. Fu Ma hesitated a few moments before joining the dark crowd making its way toward the top of the mountain. There were no lights by the path, and car headlights swept by every now and then from the mountain road, passing through the silhouetted trees and casting a shadow like moving bars, which made Fu Ma feel like he and the people around him were marching arduously, unknowingly, in an abstract prison. What a beautiful sympathy-inspiring image, he thought.

He tried to remember Grandfather again, but found that his brain was now dulled, that the flash of pure emotion for his childhood years had lasted only an instant before vanishing again. Bullshit sentimentality — Fu Ma had never had time for it anyway. Better just to keep walking, vacant and emotionless, up the mountain.

When he was halfway up the mountain, parts of the city became visible. The lights of the buildings and the flowing lines of traffic lay spread out in a classic, predictable pattern, like a minor work by an amateur photographer. Fu Ma shut his eyes, opened them again, looked as far into the distance as he could, seeing at the edge of his vision a ragged, teeming blackness — mountains, rivers, fields, trees, insects, graveyards, roads, windows, doors, faces, things gone forever, things yet to come. The darkness encompassed all these things, and all these things were swallowed by the darkness.

After gazing at this for several minutes, Fu Ma slowed his pace, feeling as if a fine rain were falling on him, or as if a cobweb had fallen on his head. He didn't know what it was. He brushed at it futilely. He stopped in his tracks, his desire to climb the mountain gone.

It was obnoxious. Even Fu Ma couldn't understand why everything, sooner or later, ended the same way, in boredom. A boredom vast as the sky, hard as an old tree root, ineluctable. If the spirit of his dead grandfather really could look after him the way it looked after others, he hoped it would protect him from boredom, would see to it that he could be like the others, could always appear full of energy.

Fu Ma felt in his pocket, but he'd smoked all of his cigarettes. There was only his phone. He took it out, unhappily, and flicked back to the Timer function, hit the Start button. He turned around listlessly and walked back through the crowd, against the flow of the half-lit, rising and falling silhouettes, back down the mountain. He put the phone back in his pants pocket, letting the numbers flip past, like ants, second after biting second.

THE PAST OF
XU'S DUCK

Translated by **Jeremy Tiang**

If I hadn't died, the longest surviving duck shop on Nanjing's Shuiximen would surely have been mine, Xu's Duck. For all I know, there might even have been branches, or a franchise. I'd have made my mark. This isn't just me bragging — back in the day, all my regulars said so too. On evenings in high summer, when the streets had been sprinkled with water, a sultry haze wavering in the twilight, two or three old guys would sit around with their upper bodies bare, snacking on "four duck parts" (two wings and two feet) as they enjoyed their liquor, slurping half a cup at a gulp — and someone would always say that with a sigh. To this day, they still miss Xu's Duck.

That's right, more than twenty years ago, Xu's Duck was fairly famous around Shuiximen, about as well-known as Shuiximen Yin's Duck, Shuiximen Cheng's Duck, Shuiximen Lu's Duck and so on — everyone claimed to sell authentic Shuiximen Salted Duck. As long as you had "Shuiximen" in your shop name, business was unbelievably good, especially in the afternoon. I opened promptly at half past three, and every single day a line would form before three o'clock. My assistant and I worked non-stop, one of us chopping up ducks and the other serving customers, and we'd be sold out by six, leaving the glass display shelf empty and glistening beneath the greasy shaded lamp. It was the same with the other shops. Nanjing people just adore eating duck, you see, it's like they've been bewitched — rich or poor, in company or alone, in hot weather or cold, with congee or strong drink. It felt like a sin not to eat duck at least once a day.

When it came to duck, there were so many culinary varieties it was hard to know how to choose. All the businesses, big and small, went along with this trend — struggling to find their own niche, marked with exquisite delicacy. A single duck would be dismembered to be stewed or roasted or smoked or air-dried or salted, served everywhere from big banquets to alleyway stalls, in scores of different styles.

Our ducks were so good because I knew how to suffer. Never mind anything else, let's just take rubbing them with salt. Everyone else wore rubber gloves for this step, but I never did, not even on the coldest days of the year. I worried gloves would decrease the sensation in my fingers, and the salt would spread unevenly, or even leave behind a rubbery taste. Salted duck takes on flavors easily because its flesh is soft and tender, so I took special care on this point. I also never used a plastic basin, for fear it would taint the flavor. My nose was very sensitive, and I only had to take one sniff of another restaurant's duck to know if they'd soaked it in old brine or fresh! Oh, sorry, I've gone off the point. Dead people are lonely, so we grow talkative. Anyway, I always used my bare hands for the salt-rubbing stage, treating my ducks like tiny women, gently stroking their skin and caressing their flesh, massaging them inside and out, servicing them so evenly, till they were bright and fragrant! A shame it left my hands stingingly reddened, swollen and too unbearably painful to be touched. But the more agony these hands of mine were in, the tastier our Xu's ducks were, and the more I could be sure the whole family would remain well-fed.

So I made sure our bellies stayed full, and as for my wife, she kept all of us well-clothed. She was a salesgirl at the state-run Taichang Fabric Store. Everyone in old Nanjing knew that Taichang's employees had a reputation for being neat, slim, and silver-tongued. Beautiful women have an advantage in business, especially when what they're selling is cloth! My wife didn't speak much, nothing outstanding in that department, but she had her own knack – with a thin, patterned piece of material, she'd nimbly shake it out and drape it across her neck so it fell at an elegant angle, causing customers to clap their hands in delight and immediately demand a piece, while with thicker, navy blue cloth, her practiced hands would fold it twice on a slant, then place it on her shoulder like the boxy collar of a suit, smiling sweetly so even old geezers with one foot in the grave would reach for their wallets!

The best thing about working at the shop was that she frequently got to take home unwanted goods. The business ordered cloth by the bolt, each of which would have little defects at either end of the roll that couldn't be placed on sale, so instead were offered to employees at half price. My wife often came home with her arms full of fabric, and that very night she'd stay up late at her sewing machine. The next day, there'd be an absolutely gorgeous jacket.

Oh, one more thing – my wife suffered from body odor. That's something I never told anyone when I was alive. But think about it, if not for this little defect, a duck-seller like me would never have been allowed to adore her. No one else knew what was going on under her armpits, and I didn't mind. In fact, it made me love her even more. As she lay in my arms every night, I wanted to hold onto her my whole life. She was so delicate and soft in my embrace, making me seem all the more coarse.

Everything ought to have continued smoothly. I'd have kept selling my duck, slowly working Xu's Duck up to the number one business on Shuiximen Street. My wife should have gone on selling fabric until Taichang went bankrupt five years later. But things didn't turn out like that.

My meek little missus, without saying a word, made a cuckold of me.

In the end, it was Boss Qian, the Pan-Fried Bun King from across the road, who told me about it. We came from the same hometown, and we got on well. He was behaving strangely that day, suddenly showing up looking all solemn in a herringbone gabardine-blend waistcoat, saying he wanted to "have a few words." I chuckled when I saw him, because I immediately recognized that his woolen waistcoat was made of rejected cloth from my wife's shop, sold at a seventy percent discount — that was practically giving it away! She got just enough material to make me and him a waistcoat each. Seeing me point at the waistcoat and laugh, Boss Qian pointed at it too, but remained poker-faced, making him look like he was swearing an oath on the garment — that I was a certified cuckold.

I glared at him, feeling empty at those shameless days gone by. These rumors might have already made the rounds of Shuiximen Street a dozen times, turning seven or eight corners, through the premises of Yin's Duck and Cheng's Duck with their old-or fresh-brined wares, into thousands of households, so everyone could gulp it down and poop it out, maggots sprouting in their yellow shit, leaving just me, the green-eyed fly, buzzing about pleasing customers and chopping up ducks.

Do you know, I'd always played the tough guy, my chest filled with flames or else a knife clutched close. My temper was known for many streets around, so when any of the nearby shops, including my colleagues and rivals, had any problems from bad elements, I'd stick my neck out to get them out of trouble. All in all, I counted as somebody, more or less, around Shuiximen.

So just think about it. How could I swallow this insult? But I wasn't going to take out my rage on my poor wife and let that be the end of it. In any case, I couldn't make myself lay a finger on her. That meant I'd have to go find the other man.

According to Boss Qian, I'd met the philanderer before — it was that day, when I went to the cloth shop to get that rejected herringbone gabardine cloth. When I spoke to my wife at the front counter, she pointed across the store and said, her voice full of gratitude, "There, that's Mr Yang, second-in-command of this store. He was the one who managed to get me this fabric!"

I looked in the direction of her finger. The great hall of the cloth shop was almost full of women, old and young, fat and thin, all brightly dressed. In their midst, the lone man was immediately visible. He wore a peaked cap, hands clasped behind his back, pacing slowly as he made a round of the room. Even from the back, he gave the impression of enormous dignity.

Since I'd come all the way here, I thought I might as well say hi. After all, I was the boss of Xu's Duck!

"Mr Yang!" I took it upon myself to yell.

The manager heard me and paused for a moment, but didn't

look back. Instead, he continued on his rounds, not even speeding up, another half circle before he turned round to where we were. It looked like he was approaching not because I'd called, but because his orbit just happened to bring him there. Finally, I saw what he looked like — medium height, glasses, unsmiling.

My wife introduced me to him, stammering a little. Now he changed his posture, standing like Premier Zhou Enlai, one arm half-raised and slightly bent, the other reaching forward to shake my hand warmly. I felt a little awkward — my palms were coarse from handling ducks all day. Stooping ingratiatingly, I asked, "Mr Yang, what kind of duck do you like to eat? Roast or salted or dried? I'll send some round for you to try."

We were only halfway through our handshake, but he abruptly pulled his arm away and, eyes flashing, interrupted me with a stern lecture. "Remember this. I've never accepted anything from my employees or their families. It would go against our company discipline to get in through the back door by sending gifts or treats, any of those tricks." With that, his eyes slid off my face, moving smoothly to his left cuff.

Following his gaze, I noticed a tiny clump of gray thread on his sleeve, no bigger than a mung bean. Nothing could be more natural in a cloth shop, but Mr Yang's forehead furrowed, and he swiftly pinched it up with disgust, flinging it far from him, then inspected himself all over, his shoulders and elbows and armpits, to ensure there were no other aberrations, before once again clasping his hands behind his back. He didn't look back at my face, but turned to continue his rounds, neither fast nor slow.

After Boss Qian broke the news of the affair to me, I thought back and wondered if those two were already together at that time. Why else had we received this special treatment, a piece of herringbone cloth large enough for two waistcoats, at such a steep discount? But how could I have known that at the time? I remember freezing where I stood, my hand shrinking back to my side, thoroughly stunned by his officious air and authority, filled with both respect and pity. So he didn't want to eat Xu's duck? But it was delicious! Such a shame.

How could I have known that what he really wanted to take a bite out of was my wife? When I got the news, I went to see him that same day at noon. I'd already learned that Mr Yang went home every lunchtime for a nap. Luckily, this worked well with my schedule — when I was done dealing with him, I'd still be able to get to my shop before half past three. It was important to start early in the afternoon in order to finish quickly, otherwise sales could easily grow sluggish, dragging on till six or seven with a few ducks still left on the shelf, which would be far too embarrassing a scenario for Xu's Duck. No matter what, I had to get back by three thirty.

After double-checking the number, I hammered and kicked at the door, making enough noise to bring down the roof. My heart was throbbing so hard, as if a hundred tigers were fighting to get out. Every second felt like an eternity.

From within came panicked footsteps, and the door opened a crack. The esteemed Mr Yang, who hadn't even stopped to put on his glasses, glared at me, the whites of his eyes rolling up. "Do you have the wrong house?"

"Not at all. You're just the casanova I was looking for!" I savagely shoved him aside and barged in, feeling as if I really were a ferocious tiger coming down from the mountain. I thought with delight that by the looks of things, it wouldn't take more than ten minutes to sort this out.

He did his part too. As if a storm were coming, he hurriedly slammed the door shut behind me, then rushed to close the balcony, bathroom, and kitchen windows, quickly sprinting round the house to make sure everything was sealed tight — afraid that sound would escape the house. Just as well!

As he busied himself with the windows, I took the opportunity to destroy things, smashing whatever looked the most classy and expensive.

He'd put on his glasses by then. Still, in his rumpled pajamas, he was hardly the dignified figure of our previous encounter. Watching my vandalism, his arms were like broken wings, reaching out then flopping back down. He wasn't trying to stop me, but to help — whatever I wanted to break, he would quickly hand over.

With him being so obliging, I quickly ran out of steam. After a few more items, I slumped down on the sofa, allowing myself to put my feet up.

He stood, arms drooping, waiting to make sure I wasn't going to do anything else, then shuffling to the kitchen in his slippers and reappearing with two cups of tea. "All right now?"

I jumped to my feet. "Damn! You think I just came here to smash up your house?"

He didn't understand. "What, then?" After a pause, he suddenly recalled that we hadn't properly greeted each other. "And may I ask your name?" He looked about to stick out a hand.

"I'm her husband! The duck-seller! We've met! We even shook hands!" Even with anger drumming at my heart, I could see he needed more details to remind him. "It was the day we got the

cheap herringbone gabardine, a seventy percent discount. I came
to get—"

Seeming to grow even more confused, he cut me off with a
cadre-like gesture. "They all get cloth from me. I've given all of
them discounted goods, and many times it's the husband who
comes to collect." He looked troubled, as if he was eager to clear
this up too.

This son of a bitch. This shameless hooligan. How many
discounted goods had he given to how many employees? From
satin to dacron, from polyester to gabardine, from pure wool to
acrylic blends, from camlet to lace.

"A word of advice, little brother. No use banging your head
against a brick wall. I've never taken any of this seriously, and neither
have these women. Even their husbands don't care. There's really
no need to overreact!" He waved expansively, as if to include all
the beautiful employees of Taichang Fabric Store and their spouses
within his arms. I was the only one outside his reach. His expression
said he thought I didn't know much about the world.

"Excellent, then I'm here today to settle scores on behalf of
all their husbands!" It seemed my visit today would definitely be
worthwhile. After this, the whole neighborhood would have to
respect me. I was restoring justice to the world. Hot blood burned
a pathway as it surged to my brain, setting it abuzz. I lunged over
and grabbed his collar, hoisting him off the ground like a duck.
If we'd been in my backyard, with water seething in my four-foot
metal pot, I'd have chucked him in and plucked his feathers before
anything else.

Still, he was much heavier than a duck, so after holding him up
for a short while, I ran out of energy and let him drop, kicking his

calves out from under him so he dropped into a kneeling position. He awkwardly cleared away the debris beneath his knees, and like an obedient grandson, meekly asked, "What on earth do you want?"

I said nothing. He must have thought he had some wiggle room, so shuffled on his knees closer to me, and said in an intimate tone, "Why don't I help you think of some ideas?" He started counting on his fingers. "I have quite a bit of money saved, I can give you the whole lot! To be honest, when you're in a position like mine, you can always get hold of some cash."

"Do you have preschoolers? I can get them into Drum Tower Kindergarten. That's the best one in Nanjing. They have all sorts of people knocking at their doors!"

"I'm the chair of the workers union, in charge of employee benefits. I could buy a whole lot of ducks! We'd give them out at Midautumn Festival, New Year's, and the Dragon Boat Festival, and all from your shop."

He suddenly looked transfixed. "I remember now, one of my workers gave me a salted duck once! You see, I remembered in the end! Your wife suffers from body odor, isn't that right?"

He smiled ingratiatingly — he certainly didn't look down on my wife.

I grabbed my cup of tea (if only it was still scalding!) and flung it at his face, leaving tea leaves on his Don Juan nose and causing the hair at his temples to hang down, dripping. In shock, he knelt straighter, as if better posture might affect his fate. Like a sunflower, his head tilted as his eyes followed my every move. Uncomprehending, he asked, "Don't you like any of these offers? I could even do all three—"

"Three hundred wouldn't do you any good! You fucked my wife!" I stormed, pacing around him.

"You tell me then, what do you want?" He bit his lip, and said nothing more.

That was a good question — what did I want? How would I get my revenge on this bastard? This was different from dealing with those street ruffians. I had a hazy, looming goal – to punish him in a most unusual way, so he felt he might as well be dead.

The house felt too quiet, with only the ticking of the wall clock to be heard, as I scrunched up my face in thought. At this point, my brain held just one idea, which was also the most immediate one.

The man at my feet had clearly reached the same conclusion. Sighing lightly, he said, "I get it. You want my life."

Before leaving home, I'd tucked a small blade into my jacket, something I'd used for many years, about the size of a shaving razor. A duck's throat isn't very thick, after all. You pinion its wings back with your left hand, and with your right pull its head back and tuck it beneath those wings, so the long, curved neck is bared. The blade, held at an angle, scrapes off the fine hairs, then you push it straight in, and it's over in two seconds. Next, you hang the carcass upside down, so the brownish-red duck blood can trickle out into a basin. There are people who go door to door collecting that blood.

Casanova stared at my hands, but they remained where they were for now. It only took two seconds. I was in no hurry.

"You're simply a duck-slaughterer. How intelligent could you be? I knew it would be something corny like this! If that's what you want, then I have nothing to say. I couldn't beat you in a fight."

With a show of solemnity, he shut his eyes, as if in prayer. At the same time, I detected a sharp odor, even nastier than a duck's butt

— the son of a bitch had wet himself. This scum was even worse than a duck.

I didn't mind the smell of piss, what I did mind was the implication that I was a brainless thug who relied on my strength to bully others. That wasn't a good look on me. If word got out, it wouldn't sound great. I made a quick decision — not to cut him, but to think of something more unpredictable.

"I wouldn't dirty my knife on a coward like you!" I was happy to talk like a real tough guy. "I want you to go on suffering! I'm going to destroy your life. You'll beg for merciful death." Although the words tripped off my tongue, my mind was still in knots. How was I going to come up with a plan to fix him?

The philanderer slowly opened his eyes, like a gambling addict looking at all his cards and seeing that, against the odds, he'd actually won this hand. Steadying himself, he instantly switched to his managerial voice in order to praise me. "I see I was wrong about you. You have a great future ahead of you! I promised you mountains of gold and silver just now, and you refused all those riches, which earned my admiration. I deliberately asked you to kill me, but if you did that you would lose your own life as well — you'd have harmed me without benefiting yourself. And you saw through that trick too."

He shook his head and sighed, not taking his eyes off me. I could practically hear the gears in his head turning. My gaze was fixed at him too, pretending to think too — whichever one of us came up with an idea first would be in charge.

His voice turned gentle. "I guess you don't want to settle this between you and me? You're thinking you might make an official complaint to the store, am I right?"

What was he doing, one foot here and one foot there, kicking around the idea of my revenge? When he talked about murder, at least that was a desirable plan. But now this talk of official complaints — that wasn't something that had crossed my mind.

He patiently explained, "That's right, I'm a state employee. If you bring this to the higher-ups, that'd be a serious lifestyle violation, and I'd be finished, completely wiped out. Reduced to nothing, overnight. I joined the store as an apprentice, aged twelve, and it took me twenty-seven years to become a model worker, then a cadre, and finally a deputy manager. It's been half a lifetime. You can't imagine how much I've had to put up with."

Did he think he'd encountered a soulmate? Now he was opening his heart, confiding his past to me, interspersing his story with many vivid examples of how he'd suffered.

I couldn't interrupt him, and I had to admit he had the gift of the gab. I found myself sympathizing with him. It sounded like the road to an official position wasn't much better than being a duck-seller. My hot blood started to cool. He concluded, "That would be a cruel thing to do — you'd completely ruin me."

I felt a jolt of joy as I recalled our first encounter — how he'd fastidiously flicked that clump of thread off his shirt with his fingertips. This sort of person valued his reputation and rank much more than his life. In which case, checkmate! I'd land him in deep shit. I'd bring him down!

Seeing me relax, he stood up without asking, as if he'd completed his mission. He even patted the dust off his knees, and urged, "So we're done here?"

I didn't answer right away. The tone of his voice was disturbing me.

He picked up the other teacup and took a large gulp of the tea I hadn't flung in his face. "Ah, little brother, my good fellow, Mr. Duck-seller." He was talking to me in a casual manner, like a close friend. "You know, I'm also in charge of the workers union, which means I've had to deal with far too many domestic trifles like this. Every useless small potato has the same idea you did — go talk to the boss, to management, to the higher-ups! What's the use? A perfectly manageable little affair suddenly becomes a big deal, to be discussed in public meetings and recorded in official documents!"

He shook his head, one hand first slapping his thigh, then coming to rest on my shoulder. Even though he was still in his pajamas, he was beginning to resemble a leader. "How foolish! What are your superiors? What is the organization? People, that's what! It's all people, with ears and mouths and you-know-what in their bowels. All of those shameful things — when you report them, you'll have to talk about them. When they investigate, they'll ask you again. When they're negotiating how to deal with the situation, they'll talk about it many more times. And when the outcome is announced, they'll have to sum up the whole matter, and that'll cause comment in public, several hundred times. Round and round it goes. Let's say I slept with your wife a dozen or so times. By the time this gets into people's mouths, your wife will have jumped in and out of my bed hundreds, maybe thousands of times! In the end, think about it, you'll have destroyed my reputation, I'll admit that, but you'll have wrecked your wife's too, as well as Xu's Duck — who'd still buy anything from you? You'd be placed in the limelight and become a laughing stock! In the end, you'd be the biggest loser."

Hearing him denigrate Xu's Duck like that sent a sharp jolt of pain straight through me, and I had a vivid image of people pointing and gossiping about me. He was a persuasive speaker. His words froze me, turning my brain into mush. If I'd cooled down before, now I was on ice. The way he put it, I was completely helpless. I could neither kill him nor expose him. My only choice was to pretend ignorance, just like all the other husbands, sneak back home in dejection, and continue getting unwanted fabric to make waistcoats with.

Tick tock, tick tock. I looked up at the clock. It was almost two, and I'd accomplished nothing! Had I barged in here just to chat with him? The flames that had just died down in my head flared back to life. I lashed out at the clock, knocking it to the ground and stamping it into smithereens. All its little gears tumbled out, and its springs bounced here and there. That noisy second hand was quiet now.

"Shut up, that's enough stupid ideas from you! You think I'm some elementary school student, reporting you to the teacher? We're going to sort this out between us, you and I, man to man!" I screamed, in a proper rage now, spraying his face with saliva. Of course, I was aware that after what he'd said, I didn't have many options left. What a situation to be in!

"You tell me, then. I'll do whatever you say." He seemed to have run out of energy. His shoulders sagged in defeat.

Huh, with time so tight, how could I think? I told him to kneel down again, and slapped him a couple of times, once on either side. "This is your mess, you bastard, and you'll have to clear it up yourself. Listen carefully. My demands are very simple. I want to take my anger out on you! Do you know what it feels like to have someone sleep with your wife? Hmm? I need to think of a way so you'll feel as mad as me, like your belly's on fire, like you

75

want to gnash your teeth into pieces and swallow the stumps." After thinking about it a moment, I added a condition, "Whatever you come up with, my wife, myself, and my Xu's Duck shop, can't be harmed at all!"

That son of a bitch was bleeding from the mouth now, swirling it between his teeth, not daring to spit. He mumbled what I'd said, "You vent, I suffer, so I'm the same as you." Looking at me ingratiatingly, he pleaded, "And you don't want money, nor anything public, this has to be between us."

I nodded, and glanced at the clock on the floor. "Hurry up! I need to be at my shop by half past three." Flames licked at my heart. I was on horseback, wielding my whip and brandishing my sword, but unable to strike. If he could think of an absolutely watertight method, I'd help him to his feet and formally thank him.

Suddenly, his head snapped round. I heard a gurgle in his throat as he swallowed the blood in his mouth, and perhaps a broken tooth, too. His face was waxy and pale, like a living corpse. I started feeling good about myself. Whatever he said next would surely be worth hearing. I bent down and drew closer. When I looked at his left side, he twisted right, but when I switched to his right, he flinched left.

The living corpse opened its mouth. "The way I see it, there's only one choice — you'll have to sleep with my wife."

I got goose bumps all over my body.

As soon as the words were out, he wobbled to his feet, leaning against the doorframe as he headed to the bathroom to clean his face, then hurrying to the bedroom to change into his work clothes. When he reappeared, his head was still tilted like a zombie's, not looking at me, spitting out the words like nails. "This way, we'll be even. All debts canceled." Like three red stamps at the bottom of a contract.

I burst out laughing, so loudly I doubt those doors and windows could have kept the noise in. What a splendid idea — simple, rational, and fair. This bastard really was talented. I was overjoyed, still chortling as I looked at him. This provincial model worker, this Mr Yang, manager, and also chair of the workers union — how I enjoyed seeing him like this, impeccably dressed and completely lifeless. Look at him, about to undergo the same humiliation I'd suffered. His wife was about to sleep with another man. Damn it, what a perfect outcome. I hadn't seen so much as a hair on his wife's head, and a third of my anger was already gone!

"Deal. Where and when?" Like him, I wasn't going to say any more than necessary. This felt good, like we were concluding an important negotiation.

Mr Yang looked at his watch. He stood staring at it for a good while, as if he hated the thing on his wrist, yet was glad he owned it. A full minute later, he finally seemed able to tell the time, and replied, "She'll be home in fifteen minutes. That's good timing. You'll be able to make it to your duck shop by half past three."

"She's agreeable?" I realized just in time that his wife didn't know anything about our arrangement. I'd only intended to deal with this casanova, and our stand-off had lasted an hour or so now. The rest needed to be simple. The last thing I wanted was a repeat session with the woman.

"I'll deal with that," said Mr Yang, heading for the door. "I'll meet her on the way, then go off to work. I'll leave my key." He fumbled in his pockets in a flurry till he found his key and tossed it to me, as if this were my place and he was the intruder.

Once he'd gotten the door open, he turned back to look at me, a weird expression on his face, as if I weren't human, but some object or creature. His expression was cold, yet at ease. It shook me so much I stayed frozen in the middle of the room for quite a while before suddenly realizing that I ought to go out to the balcony to look for a mop to wipe up his piss from next to the sofa.

For the first half of the afternoon, I'd been gripped by an urgent, impatient need for revenge, then the son of a bitch kept rambling, twisting things here and there, leaving me exhausted. I should have used this break to catch my breath and prepare for the next bout of battle. To be frank, I was full of excitement — steeped in the pleasure and desire of having found a foolproof strategy, like a starving man preparing for a feast.

Working quickly, I finished mopping the living room in ten minutes, and even cleared away the broken glass and other debris. I wasn't being conscientious. There was just no way I could have sat still at that moment.

This was the first time in my life I was waiting for someone or something like this. Sleeping with another man's wife — something I'd never considered, not till ten minutes ago. What a thrill!

I lit a cigarette, but had forgotten how to smoke. Think about it, while I was holding this cigarette, on the busy road outside, Mr Yang was waylaying his wife, dragging her to the shade of a tree, where they wouldn't be overheard — I could imagine all this, but not what came next. How would he explain this to her? What sort of woman was she? How would she react?

Without meaning to, I began speculating about this unknown Mrs Yang. Standing on the balcony, I looked down at the alleyway below. All kinds of women were passing by. Some tall, some wearing those greasy blue sleeve protectors, some bowlegged, some so fat they might as well have been two people. One of them got into an argument with a rag-and-bone man over ten cents. I stayed there a while, studying them all closely.

None of them were right. I shook my head, jeering at myself. Mr Yang, deputy store manager and chair of the workers union, would definitely have a different sort of wife. She may well be a theater announcer, long-haired and in a long gown. I'd never seen one of them off stage. Or perhaps a lady cadre, all proper with her hair in a bob? If she was as glib as him, I'd be in trouble — she'd surely come up with some big theories! I'd rather she were a kindergarten teacher, someone who could chant nursery rhymes and play children's games, her hands soft and voice tender. Of course, all possibilities boiled down to the same question — no matter what sort of woman she was, how would she feel about what the two of us were going to do next? If she just balked, shied away, and wept, that would be easy enough to deal with, but what if she got hysterical and made a fuss? Or got violent, or tried to kill herself, or even phoned the police?

I was at my wits' end. There were many possibilities for how this confrontation could go. Some made me feel stressed and unhappy, others left me chuckling. Then I burned my finger on the end of the cigarette, and the pain jolted me back to myself. Hadn't I just talked this over with her husband? I was going to fuck his wife. That was that — why bother so much thinking about it? It didn't matter what she did. I wouldn't care. On behalf of all the cuckolds in the world, I was going to fight a fierce battle. I'd fight as hard as fifty men, and if anyone suffered, it would be that bastard.

Slapping my palm on my chest, a cigarette bobbing from one corner of my mouth, I felt as if I'd suddenly grown larger, eager now to taste the meat of vengeance, to sip its heady wine.

Entering the bedroom, I tilted my head as I studied the double bed. On the bedside table was a small jar of cold cream. Walking over, I twisted off its lid. Whether because of my wife's body odor or my shop reeking of duck, I had a peculiar fondness for all kinds of fragrances, especially the lotions women smear on their faces, hands, lips, or hair. As I sat on the edge of the bed and held the open jar to my nose, the front door suddenly clicked open.

Jar in one hand, lid in the other, I quickly tried to jam them together, but the lid was somehow too small and slid off, skittering across the floor. A woman stood in the doorway, completely still. The two of us listened to the lid rolling along, until it finally came to a halt somewhere under the bed.What was that woman standing in front of me like? Attractive or hideous? What sort of temperament? Was she about to cause trouble? I stared at her unblinkingly, but couldn't answer any of those questions, couldn't even make out her features. It was as if she'd arrived wrapped in a giant sack so I could only make out a vague impression – gray and limp, no vitality to her at all.

She didn't move till the lid came to a halt, at which point she set down her two bags, which were stuffed full of mundane objects, lunch boxes and towels, potatoes and cabbages. Still silent, she took off her shoes and put on house slippers, washed her hands, then walked into the bedroom, went to the side of the bed, and immediately took off her jacket.

Stunned, I stood up, still holding that lidless jar of cold cream.

She swiftly removed her trousers too. Looking tired, she crawled into bed, as if she needed to lie down before she felt strong enough to say something. Up till now, she hadn't so much as glanced at me.

Speaking into the air, without any hatred or repulsion on her face, she said, "This is when I normally go to sleep. I'm the night nurse at the hospital. I started work at eleven last night. Just me, in charge of three patients — they all arrived in the small hours of the morning. We struggled all night. Now two are dead, one's still alive. Forty minutes on a crowded bus to get here, then I stopped at the market for groceries. You'd better hurry up. I'm exhausted." Her voice was uninflected, neither warm nor cold. How strange that a human being could talk like that.

Seeing that I hadn't moved, she went on, "Are you waiting for me to clean up? I had a shower at the hospital. Look, my hair's still damp. Go ahead. Don't you have to leave by three thirty?" It was as if she was pouring a cup of tea to get rid of a beggar, urging him to quickly drink it up while it was hot, then be on his way as soon as possible.

Was this it? Was this really Mr Yang's wife? Or had he gone out and hired some woman to play this part? How shameless. What kind of revenge was this? How was this meant to make me feel better? I was shocked and full of anger, a great hole punctured in my sense of satisfaction.

What had gone wrong? I didn't understand! This was the right situation, everything was going according to plan — I'd made an arrangement with her husband, and he'd obviously explained everything to her, and now she was waiting for me to sleep with her. Wasn't that the plan?

The woman kept removing her clothes as I watched, stripping

to her cotton singlet and floral panties, then burrowing beneath the covers, piling the discarded clothes on the bedside table. I suddenly noticed an aroma on the sweater she'd just removed. It was exactly the same as the jar of cold cream.

Completely inappropriately, my wife popped into my head. I've said she suffered from body odor, and also how that made me love her even more. Of course, I must admit, those with this affliction are most afraid of the moment they have to take off their clothes, to expose their armpits so a day's worth of perspiration is suddenly released, a stinky balloon popping, leaving even someone like me, surrounded by ducks all day, reeling from the stench. This woman smelled delightful. Yet the awful thing was, when I looked at her wooden face, all of that fragrance turned sour!

I stayed where I was. She thought about it, then laughed dryly, forcefully. "Heh, don't tell me you're shy? You know how many men we nurses see? Old and young, half-dead, all day long we wipe them down and fit them with catheters. If they have bladder cancer, the piss doesn't come — we have to massage it out of them. Heh." She lay down. "I'm shattered! I'll wait a few minutes more, but don't blame me if I fall asleep. Of course, heh, you shouldn't let that stop you either, you know what I mean?"

I took a couple of steps back, moving away from the bed. I'm no fool, and knew she wasn't really that tired or drowsy. This was some kind of cheap trick to get things over with as quickly as possible. But now this idiotic woman had made the whole situation disgusting.

Now I missed the clock I'd smashed, the one now sitting in the trash. If only it was still hanging on the wall, I'd be able to turn back time, back to when I'd just burst into the house, while I was still breaking things, while that son of a bitch was kneeling and making me offers. I'm not saying I regretted my decisions. I just mean I really missed that clock. I longed for the time it once pointed to.

"Are you embarrassed?" The woman suddenly looked me up and down, her eyes as filthy as a mouthful of spit. I instinctively shrank into myself. In a pinched voice, she asked excitedly, "Do you know how my man fucked your wife? Huh?"

That was a detail I hadn't asked for. I didn't want to talk about it.

"During the evening shift! It's a state-owned business, so they stop work at nine, and that's when the late shift finishes. Usually, there are hardly any customers that late, so no one would care if one of the salesgirls disappeared for twenty minutes." She didn't even pause to draw breath, as if her words would dry up if she stopped. "There's nothing in the back room of Taichang except bales and bales of cloth. You could fuck anywhere in there! In the stock room, on old counters, in the corridors. He has the key to the stock room. Just imagine how convenient that is. Material piled so high, wide and soft, perfect for fucking on. He'd pick whichever girl wasn't doing anything, beckon her over, say he needed her for a character-building exercise."

Now I recalled that when I'd gone to pick up the herringbone gabardine, I'd passed through the stock room. It was dark and cramped in there, full of nooks and crannies, smelling of old fabric. After what she'd said, I suddenly saw my wife clearly, her thighs bare, pressed between two rolls of cloth by Mr Yang, the man's shirt and tie still impeccably neat. At his ease, so conveniently, he fucked her, now forcing my wife's legs higher, now flipping her onto her front, all the while chatting casually about her service attitude, the productivity competition, the model worker contest. In time with

Mr Yang's rhythm, the large bales of fabric trembled against each other, like the keyboard of an accordion, slowly swaying this way and that, a silent accompaniment.

Goddammit, I didn't need to see that. Why was this damn woman bringing all this up? Wasn't this already shameful enough? If she didn't shut up I was going to thrash her.

She barked out a sneering little laugh. "Heh, at least one husband's turned up to settle scores with him." She looked at me, almost grateful, and twitched aside the blanket to beckon me. Without my noticing, she'd slipped off her underwear, and her naked body flashed blindingly at me. I noticed that her legs were curved, splayed open, completely symmetrical. She was in position, like a smoked and air-dried white-fleshed duck.

Thinking of ducks made me remember the time. I had no idea how long I'd been here. My god, I had to get back punctually. When it came to the duck business, I was very competitive. All these years, no matter what happened, appendectomies or broken legs or my grandmother dying, Xu's Duck had been the first of the duck shops to open every day, and that afternoon was going to be no exception.

With that thought, I ordered myself to take off my own clothes. It hadn't been easy to come up with this plan, and even if this really had been an air-dried duck laid out before me, I'd still have been obliged to mount it.

As soon as I lay down, she took the initiative to wrap herself around me. Her arms were cold, the scent of cold cream stronger on her body. In that brightly-lit room, we looked like an old couple, completely unembarrassed. I finally managed to make out the woman in front of me. She was pale and short, her hair sparse. Not pretty enough, but with an intelligent face, the intelligence of self-abandonment.

She drew a little closer, preventing me from looking directly at her, as if we really did know each other intimately. "I go out every night before he gets back from the late shift. I reach home at this time every day, right after he leaves after his nap. We're never in bed at the same time. I clean myself thoroughly after work every day. I even think I'm too clean." She looked at me entreatingly.

Her words sent a pang through my heart, and I almost hugged her back. But I stopped myself, and instead felt a deep wave of humiliation at this pain. This woman was actually talking to me, baring her heart! I'd almost pitied her! What was this? If she was crazy, then so was I.

I pushed her away, forcing her to look me in the eye, and glared at her. She immediately smiled joyfully at me, as if not at all bothered by how we'd come to be here, but happy to enjoy the moment and fuck me thoroughly. This was taking the illusion too far — it was all so much horseshit, and I wasn't going to put up with it. Even worse, I could see myself through her eyes, someone about the same as her, teeth clenched and putting up with it.

I couldn't help thinking of the four of us, Mr Yang, my wife, her, and me. The other two were just fine, but how had the pair of us wound up here, suffering this icy punishment?

There was simply no way I could fuck her, none at all. This was messed up.

My brain wandered backward, replaying the scenarios in slow motion a couple of times. Things had started out well, yet somehow turned a corner and ended up with this ashen woman, this limp, lifeless creature! As soon as she'd appeared, everything had gone wrong. I couldn't say exactly how, but without question, she was the one who'd ruined this! Despicable. I'd started out hating that casanova more than anyone else, but at this point, he'd dropped to second place.

The woman, not knowing any of this, was still energetically playing the coquette, even climbing on to me, her half shriveled breasts like two wounded pigeons, softly drooping down. "He stopped me in the street just now and told me about this, and I agreed without another word. I want to sleep with you. I didn't care which of his salesgirls' husbands you are. You could have been any random man from the street. As soon as I said yes, he slapped me. You see, from the tip of my ear to my neck, it's all bruised. He really hit me hard."

She pointed, and guided my left hand to her cheek and neck. Sure enough, it was faintly red, and the marks of three fingers were still visible. She stretched her neck for me to see — it was long and slender, and curved at an attractive angle. I gently stroked those three finger marks, then slowly expanded my reach, until I was caressing her entire neck, up and down, front and back, very carefully stroking it.

Her eyes reddened all of a sudden, making her look like a rabbit. She glared at me with those crimson eyes, which were slowly brimming with tears, and tried to pull my hand down to her breasts, but I wouldn't let her. It remained firmly around her neck. She trembled, like a leaf about to be blown off the tree in a gale.

"Your neck, it's pretty good." I suddenly realized that these were the first words I'd spoken to her, and thus the only words.

As soon as I opened my mouth, she understood. I didn't want her. No matter how energetically she advertised herself, it wasn't going to do any good. I didn't want her. Without a word, she slid away, her body shrinking, losing the rest of its moisture, turning completely dry. As if my rejecting her was even more humiliating than her husband rejecting her. As if I was the frost in an already harsh winter, the last straw. For some unknown reason, the more pathetic she looked, the angrier I got.

And still this stupid woman wouldn't admit defeat. She struggled to lie on her side, and quickly found her escape route, the one she'd put in place as soon as she'd stepped in the door. "I'm exhausted, anyway. I'm going to sleep now. Shut the door behind you when you leave." Her head reared up, and she smiled with the last of her energy.

"Heh, I thought this might happen! You're like my husband, you think I'm too old. For sure, I'm not as young and pretty as your wife. But—" Her head finally sank onto the pillow, and stayed still. "Let's say we did sleep together, the two of us."

The way she talked genuinely moved me. It seemed she wasn't actually so shameless as all that. Her final suggestion inspired me. Yes, I suddenly had an idea, like a bamboo shoot sprouting from the ground — it just sprang from my brain! This could get my plan back on track!

Turning around, I embraced her, this time of my own volition, encircling her icy arms from behind. At the same time, my other hand crept to the pile of clothes by the bed, and nimbly retrieved my thin, light blade. It was like dealing with a shelduck, sticking it into her. Of course, her neck wasn't a duck's, so I had to use a little more energy than normal.

Out of habit, I moved her to the side of the bed, bending her neck over the edge so it hung into space, trying not to soil the sheets. Her blood began to flow, but sluggishly. I had time to dash to the bathroom and bring back the cleanest basin I could find, which I set beneath her head.

Next, I got busy. This was at the heart of my plan, and in keeping with her suggestion. I picked up her clothes, sweater and singlet, bra and panties, and everything else, and like scattering seeds, flung them across the living room and bedroom, as if they'd been pulled off in a struggle — I even ripped some of them. Then I messed up the sheets, smearing tracks of dirt everywhere. Finally, I had to deal with her body — roughing up the relevant organs and certain other corners a fair bit, until they were in the state I imagined they'd be in after a woman had been savagely fucked by a strapping ruffian, a man smoldering with lust. I think I did all right. Hadn't Mr Yang complimented me on my intelligence? That might have been sarcasm, but it really did exist, and here I was manifesting it! I went so far as to playfully arrange her legs into the posture they'd assumed under the blankets – symmetrically splayed out, like those of a smoked and air-dried salted duck.

All this while, blood was bubbling from the woman's mouth, and her staring eyes followed me. I was too busy to pay close attention. I guessed she wouldn't blame me — she wasn't stupid, and had so much pride, she'd understand I was doing the right thing. I was helping her. This woman who'd endured repeated betrayal and abandonment, whom no one wanted, not even herself — she might as well be dead. Don't you think so?

Then I sat and waited for her to breathe her last.

As I left the bedroom, I turned back for a final look at her on the bed. I felt proud of myself. I'd done a good job.

Unexpectedly, I noticed the lid of the cold cream jar. It had come to rest at the outermost leg of the bed. Turning around, I picked it up, carefully screwed it back onto the jar, and placed it back on the bedside table. As I did this, I took another sniff at the cream. Still fragrant.

After that, I got dressed and left, shutting the door behind me. Along the way, I passed by a clock repair shop and stopped to chat with the owner, whom I knew. Asking the time, I was pleased to hear it was only a quarter past three. I hadn't missed anything at all.

I opened the shop as usual and sold ducks alongside my assistant. There was nothing out of the ordinary. By six o'clock, we were sold out, the glass display shelf gleaming greasily as always beneath the light. Ha, when we finished, Yin's Duck still had four or five birds hanging in their window.

After sending away my assistant, I brought out the half duck neck I had set aside for myself and began slowly gnawing it as I stared at my shop sign and let my mind wander.

My old customers were right. I'd always been ambitious, dreaming of making Xu's Duck the best salted duck business in all of Nanjing, with branches all the way from Confucius Temple to Hunan Road, so tourists from all over could grab half a bird to enjoy on the train. They'd definitely have loved it. What a shame.

As for my wife, there's no need to worry about her, she quietly left Taichang Fabric Store, and five years after I died, Taichang went bankrupt too — nowadays who would bother to buy cloth and make clothes on their own? By this time, the whole incident was covered in dust and buried, and no one cared, so she was able to remarry without a fuss. Her life went on untroubled.

I've thought more about Mr Yang. How can I put this? Revisiting the details of my interactions with him, I grew a little unhappy. I've thought of one reason why. Could this timid little bastard have deliberately said this and that, leading me down this path? In this way, he'd be completely safe, and his hands clean too. And he probably expected that I wouldn't be able to sleep with his wife? In any case, he'd worked it all out so he wouldn't lose anything.

No! I immediately rebuked myself. Through this whole thing, I was completely in charge. I was the one who refused his three offers. I hadn't condescended to kill him, nor make an official complaint. Instead, I negotiated this plan step by step. I firmly believed that no man on earth would be willing to offer up his wife to someone else. Every man on Shuiximen, in the whole of Nanjing, of China, of the earth, would think so too. I must absolve Mr Yang of any suspicion. Such doubts, even a hint of them, are the greatest injustice and insult to him, to me, and to all men.

Besides, as for whether or not I slept with his wife, ha ha — I have to laugh out loud when I think of this point! When the truth came out, the whole of Shuiximen was talking about it — the shops next to mine, my old hometown friends, my loyal customers, all those little ruffians and gangsters — and the main point they emphasized was my cruel, violent, creative revenge. No one would talk about how Mr Yang had got my wife into bed, all they wanted to discuss was how I'd fucked his! Esteemed Mr.Yang, deputy manager of the store and chair of the workers union, did get one thing right — all through the explanation, investigation, trial, and street rumors, I slept with his wife thousands of times. My cuckold's horns were plucked clean off and placed firmly on his head.

As for that woman, that's right, all the while I was arrested and sentenced, up to my death and then till now, after all these years, I still think of her now and then. At the end, did she understand what I did was for her own good? Anyway, I don't feel any remorse about what I did to her, nor what I didn't do. If I had a do-over, I'd still do the same, although I'd say one more thing to her. "As for you, you do have one advantage – you smell much nicer than my wife." I didn't tell her this and give her a moment of happiness. That's the one thing I do regret.

THE BANQUET

Translated by **Michael Day**

I

With grim determination, Yang Zao steeled himself to face the day. He waited on his paralyzed father, helped him with his morning bowel movement, helped him eat his breakfast, then hit the road.

He hurried down the road at a rapid clip, shoulders hunched, walking tall. He'd nearly reached his sister's house when he spotted two people he recognized at the entrance to the alley, Mr. Qian and Ms. Xiao. A few years earlier, when his sister was in the middle of a messy divorce, these two had come running to her side. Yang Zao merely clenched his jaw, showing not a hint of a smile. Yang Zao never used to act this way. When he saw someone he knew approaching, he'd start preparing a smile from far away, an orphan's smile showing deference, good cheer, and just the right amount of thankfulness, rubbing his hands together as he walked. He noticed that Mr. Qian looked taken aback, and Ms. Xiao was rubbing her eyes. He ignored them.

He knocked loudly on Yang Wan's door.

Yang Wan asked over and over if it was really him before opening up the door, then gave her brother a long, fearful look, as if he'd shown up missing an arm. His sister looked more and more like his mom. His mother had been just like this when she was alive — nerves on edge at the faintest whiff of a storm, always worried about the family's bedspreads that nobody ever aired out.

Yang Zao abruptly commanded Yang Wan to sit, and he was about to open his mouth when Yang Wan pointed to the other side of the curtain and made a *shh* sound. "He just went to sleep. Whooping cough has had him knocked out for weeks." His sister started telling him about her son, Doudou. They'd been to countless different hospitals, put him on an IV time and again, spent tons of cash, and on and on. The words were hollow, disjointed, and full of pregnant pauses.

Yang Zao lowered his head and listened to her speak. Yang Wan continued blabbing for a while until at last she could no longer hold back.

"What on earth is going on? Why did you…?"

"I've got the chance… to ask… Brother Rong… out for dinner." Yang Zao pronounced the words slowly and deliberately. He'd been holding them in all evening.

"Brother Rong?" Yang Wan hurriedly pasted a smile on her face. It was a stiff, tentative smile.

Hadn't she heard of Brother Rong? Yang Zao's nostrils flared. One, two, three. He counted silently to himself. If she reacted within three seconds, he'd let it pass.

"Oh, Brother Rong, yes, Brother Rong." Yang Wan looked away and gave a guilty nod. Damn, she really didn't get it. Yang Zao leaned in close and spelled things out for her. In a flash, she understood, and a guarded look appeared on her face. "I didn't know there were still people like that." She had a certain girlish ignorance. The world was the way it seemed; the world was the way the papers said it was.

"Of course there are! The more developed the country, the more common they are. Look how common they are in other countries. And China is getting more and more like those countries," Yang Zao explained with all the patience he could muster. He briefly explained to his sister what *The Godfather* was all about to help her understand exactly who and what Brother Rong was. Yang Wan's mouth was half open. She listened, then turned her head and started cleaning noisily. It was a one-room apartment, not even two and half meters tall, and although the light was poor, and although it was barely the size of a pigpen, it was his sister's most valuable asset, and she loved and cherished it, keeping it spotless.

She knelt down to wipe the floor, the incrimination in her tone reaching near ecstatic heights. "I'm glad that damn pig took the house. It was too big, and I would've never been able to clean it all."

Her pet name for her ex-husband was "that damn pig." That damn pig didn't pay Doudou's child support on time. Yang Zao had gone over to demand it from him on a few occasions, returning each time with another black eye. That damn pig was 1.82 meters tall.

Just watching her stubbornly wiping the floor in repetitive movements, Yang Zao started to feel tired. It hadn't been easy for a household made up of the old, the sick, and the incapable — that is, his aged father, his sister, and Doudou — to come by this refuge. There was nobody in the family he could talk business with. He closed his eyes and leaned back in the rock-hard chair, and the sense that he was an orphan came back to him. But he'd heard that in their line of work, women, children, and the elderly would always be cared for. That was the grand tradition of the "godfathers." But anyway, if there was nobody in the family he could talk business with, he'd take matters into his own hands. If his sister was too thick-headed, so be it. He'd intended to keep his plan secret anyway.

The information came from a confidential source, but as his friend put it, it was "absolutely reliable." The gist of it was that in about half a month, Brother Rong would be attending a banquet at Kaitai Restaurant, and there were still one or two empty seats. His friend could make some introductions and secure one of the seats for Yang Zao — after listening for about a minute, he saw a light shining down from the heavens, and he felt his feet lifting off the ground. This was a lot more than an opportunity to stuff a few mouthfuls of food in his mouth and wash it down with expensive liquor. He'd have to be the world's biggest fool to stop there. It was the only chance he'd ever get to have dinner with Brother Rong, and he was determined to take full advantage of this life-changing opportunity.

He stammered, timidly thanking his friend, but his heart was as cold as iron, and in an instant his mind was made up. He would pay the bill. Yes, he was going to buy dinner for Brother Rong.

Taking a gang leader out for dinner! The implications and possibilities of that both awed and frightened him. He could hardly believe it. It was like there was a red carpet rolled out for him — first, he'd make a first impression on Brother Rong. Then he'd back-scratch, boot-lick, and kiss ass like there was no tomorrow, drawing closer, begging, pleading, coming back again and again no matter how many times he was turned away. Yang Zao thought he could do it. He had to do it. As long as he finally got Brother Rong to "adopt" him, everything would be peachy keen. He'd gain power and influence, and there'd be someone to watch his back. Then he'd get all the family's problems straightened out, handling each one in order of importance, but his first priority was dealing with "that damn pig." If he missed another child support payment, he'd have Brother Rong send someone over to give him a little talking-to. That's right, they'd turn him into ground pork. That would teach that damn pig to miss his child support payments.

Behind the curtain, Doudou rolled over and launched into a coughing fit. Yang Wan hurriedly tossed down the rag, which landed in a sodden pile at Yang Zao's feet. Yang Zao kicked the rag aside and stepped forward to give his little nephew a kiss goodbye. The baby awoke and instinctively returned the kiss, trustingly wrapping its fleshy little hands around Yang Zao's neck while Yang Wan cooed in baby talk, "Uncle come see baby and baby stop coughing! Baby all better now!" This moment, its dreariness and desolation, seemed to foreshadow the life of this little baby, the heights of hope and the lows of desperation in its future. Yang Zao felt his heartbeat quicken. Yes, he had to take Brother Rong out to dinner.

The next evening, Yang Zao came home from the night shift at 11:30 to find Yang Wan waiting for him. The look on her face was like his had been the previous morning. She had something to say.

Yang Wan had brought him a lunchbox full of jiaozi, eighteen of them. She liked to use auspicious numbers when she made things. Or maybe she only did it to conceal how small the numbers were.

Their father had a voracious appetite, and he wolfed down eleven of them in seconds flat. He shoved them into his mouth, his cheek bulging out on one side as he chewed, greasy filling dripping down onto his collar and the bedspread. He couldn't blame the old man for savoring his meal. Yang Wan hadn't been in the mood to make jiaozi since the divorce.

Yang Zao took the remaining seven jiaozi into the kitchen and ate them there. He ate quickly, and Yang Wan spoke even more quickly. She managed to get out a few dozen words for each jiaozi. She'd finally figured out who Brother Rong was. She'd gotten that far, but now her head was full of a bunch of cotton-candy nonsense. For instance, she'd go with him to the dinner. Doudou would go too, and it would best if they took Dad along. Also, they had to prepare a present, something truly lavish. And after the meal, if Brother Rong wanted to partake of some "after-dinner entertainment," Yang Zao would foot the bill. All in all, they had to seize the opportunity to make this a grand occasion an unforgettable experience for Brother Rong.

"After-dinner entertainment?" That wasn't something Yang Wan would have thought of on her own. Yang Zao felt a jabbing pain in his stomach, but still he gulped down the last jiaozi. There was something he'd forgotten to tell her yesterday. The meeting with Brother Rong had to be kept strictly secret. He'd seen the look on her face and assumed his words had gone in one ear and out the other.

"Old Mr. Qian suggested it, and Ms. Xiao said the same. And they agreed to share the expenses for the after-dinner entertainment — I told them that was the condition for them going along." Yang Wan bared her teeth in an inadvertent show of pride. It wasn't a familiar expression for her, and the old, worried look returned quickly. "Have they decided on a restaurant? I want to go ask about the prices so we can get a rough idea."

Yang Zao picked up his chopsticks and banged them on the empty plate. He felt like bursting out in song, a song of rage. "So we're bringing along Doudou, and Dad, and Mr. Qian, and Ms. Xiao. You're turning Brother Rong's banquet into a vegetable market! How am I supposed to explain this to my friend?"

Yang Wan's voice sharpened, a sign that she was going to cry. "The two of them came to my house, convinced you must have brought good news. The thing about Brother Rong just slipped out, and they were falling all over themselves to get involved. It's all your fault. You're the one who just had to say hello when you saw them on the road. Also, Mr. Qian and Ms. Xiao helped me deal with that damn pig when I was getting divorced. One of them beat him up, and the other helped me get custody of Doudou. And what about you? You didn't lift a finger. You're too much of a coward."

Yang Zao stopped hitting the plate.

Yang Wan's voice gradually regained its calm. "But first things first. We'll deal with our own dilemma, and then it will be their turn — Mr. Qian wants to get signed up for a government allowance, and Ms. Xiao's son wants to pass the civil service exam. Who doesn't have something to ask of Brother Rong?"

"A government allowance! Passing the civil service exam! You do realize Brother Rong isn't the mayor?" Yang Zao felt like hitting the plate again. It amazed him how stupid people could be.

"The mayor's a nobody compared to Brother Rong. Mr. Qian and Ms. Xiao told me all about Brother Rong. Let's put it this way. Any type of problem anybody could have, from the cradle to the grave, from looking for a job to looking for a wife, or even asking the police for help to finding a doctor to finding a burial plot–"

Yang Wan paused for a moment. "It's like that movie you told me about yesterday. When nobody else can help, you can count on Brother Rong."

Those seven jiaozi were stuck in his chest. He got the feeling they always would be. "But there are only one or two empty seats."

Yang Wan smiled faintly. Obviously she'd already discussed this with Mr. Qian and Ms. Xiao. "Then we'll switch to a bigger table. The more the merrier. It'll be that much more of a grand occasion for Brother Rong. He'll love it. And anyway, we're footing the bill." From her tone, it sounded as if she knew exactly how to get on Brother Rong's good side. Yang Wan was a cashier at a supermarket, a line of work that had given her one unshakable conviction – more is better.

Resigned, Yang Zao took off his coat and went to brush his teeth. He already knew there was nothing he could say to change her mind. Yang Wan followed him into the bathroom, blabbing on. "I'll bring Doudou along. I'd like Brother Rong to be his godfather. We can gain an edge by building a solid relationship with Brother Rong – or would it be his god-grandfather? How old is Brother Rong anyway?"

"Forget about it. You know Doudou bursts out in tears at the sight of a stranger." Yang Zao spoke sharply, determined to snuff out this ridiculous idea.

In the living room, their father was beating the mattress. It looked like he'd been at it for some time already. Yang Wan rushed over to help. When she reached the doorway, she turned back and said, "Okay, have it your way. We won't bring Dad then."

When Yang Zao stepped through the doorway to his father's bedroom, the stench of vomited leeks and eggs hit him like a warm spring breeze. From the looks of it, his father had barely chewed his food. Over the next few days, Yang Zao and Yang Wan visited each other often to discuss the dinner plans. Mr. Qian and Ms. Xiao took part indirectly, making their opinions known through Yang Wan. But it was hard to speak on someone else's behalf, and more often than not the message got garbled. Yang Zao's anger gradually dissipated. Before long, the two of them showed up in person, and they formed a team of four.

There was a lot to talk about. For instance, how they would introduce themselves, who would introduce whom, what role each of them would play, what to wear, what type of present to bring for Brother Rong, and so on and so forth. The present turned out to be a contentious issue, and they spent three whole nights squabbling. Mr. Qian insisted that only something elegant and refined would do, like a painting or calligraphy scroll or some antique, while Ms. Xiao thought something practical was best – how about the latest model of cell phone? Then, on the fourth day, Yang Wan muttered some complaint under her breath, and in an instant they reached a miraculous agreement – there wouldn't be a present! None at all! The reasoned that giving a present could come across as vulgar. But Yang Zao was perfectly clear about the real reason, and so were the other three. It simply cost too much.

The debate that went on the longest was over how to handle the check. This was the point of the entire banquet, and the success or failure of Yang Zao and his team hinged on the question of when they should pay the bill and how they should pay it. They couldn't be too secretive, but it would be even worse if they were too obvious about it. They should do it in a way that showed both loyalty and a sense of humor, making a deep impression on Brother

Rong. It was quite a dilemma. After several rounds of debate, they still couldn't agree on a plan. Each time they reached a dead end, they changed the topic.

For example, when the subject of the after-dinner entertainment came up, the discussion became much more animated. Who would lead the transition, and who would serve as host? How would they know what Brother Rong liked to do? Did he like to play cards? Did he like to play sports? Did he like to play with girls?

Now that they were all beginning to trust each other, Mr. Qian and Yang Zao spoke in great depth on the subject of prostitutes, taking a disapproving tone yet showing expert knowledge. Ms. Xiao sat to one side shaking her head, and she paused meaningfully before breaking in. "Why should he give a rip about whores? Don't you think they have their fill of those in his line of work?"

Mr. Qian, who had been jabbering away enthusiastically, just stood there for a moment looking annoyed before hurriedly pasting on a smile. "You have a point. No reason to get stuck on this one idea. He's a worldly man. I guess he's had his fill of everything."

They also spent a lot of time chatting aimlessly, just to relieve the tension. Ms. Xiao liked to talk about rich, powerful people and their glamorous, dramatic lives. Mr. Qian's favorite topic was other people's misfortune, doom and disaster, and crime, which he talked about in terrifyingly lively tones. Yang Wan's depressing stories about spending all her money at the hospital, losing her wallet, and falling victim to telephone scams strained everyone's patience. But these diverse topics were interwoven like a length of braided rope, coalescing around a shared conviction — after they got on Brother Rong's good side, they'd all share in the benefits, and Brother Rong would right every wrong in each of their lives.

Their rising expectations were like a faint tune growing ever stronger, hovering in melodious coils above their heads. Beneath the evening lamplight, their shadows blended into one, growing denser, gathering strength. From time to time Doudou would cry out, and they would lower their voices. Sometimes, while the rest of them chattered away, one of them would begin to drift off to sleep. The others would shake the offender awake, mentioning the words "Brother Rong," and he or she would jolt to attention as if to a whip crack. *That's right, Brother Rong! It's almost time to invite Brother Rong out to dinner! What the hell are you thinking? Wake up!*

Throughout all this, Yang Zao paid no attention to Yang Wan. One day, after the crowd had dispersed, his throat was parched, so he asked her to bring him another glass of water. Through eyelids heavy with sleep, he noticed a change had come over Yang Wan. Her thinning hair had been dyed and done up in small bouncy reddish-brownish curls. The two moles on her left cheek had disappeared. It looked like she'd done something with her eyebrows, too. But the most conspicuous change was her teeth, which sparkled so white and bright that it almost hurt to look at them in the fluorescent light.

"What do you think you're doing?" Yang Zao was so tired he felt nauseated, and it took real effort to maintain his concentration.

"I'm watching you drink water." Along with all the other changes, her attitude had sharpened. He'd never heard her talk like that before. Her eyes stared off into distant fantasies. "A bilingual kindergarten, a bilingual elementary school. Maybe little Doudou can even go to middle school in America. I'm just worried I couldn't stand to see him go."

Noticing that Yang Zao was still staring, she came to her senses, tilting her head to the side. "What do you think of my new look? I'm pretty pleased with it myself. My guess is that Brother Rong doesn't like his girls too young." She didn't seem to notice that Yang Zao nearly spat his mouthful of water in her face. "Even Ms. Xiao is trying to lose weight, but she's 42. And I'm the one who's single."

"Don't you and Ms. Xiao ever use your brain? You don't really think Brother Rong will–" He hurriedly gulped down his water. His stomach was doing flips.

"Oh, it doesn't hurt to make a plan, just in case. What do you think of this?" Yang Wan pulled out a hairpin encrusted with fake diamonds, inserted it carefully above her forehead, and wiggled it into place so that the jewels sparkled precisely three-quarters of the way across her forehead. Now the diamonds sparkled along with her teeth. She practiced flashing a seductive smile. "This should make heads turn, don't you think?"

"Why don't you bring Doudou along? That'll make heads turn for sure," Yang Zao said sarcastically.

"That's exactly what I'm going to do." Yang Wan spoke calmly, extracting the hairpin with great care. "The other two are both bringing guests. We'll lose out if we don't do the same."

Imagine that, they were bringing guests! With all his might, Yang Zao forced his eyes open, emerging from near sleep into a throbbing headache. Yang Wan's voice sounded far away.

"Who are you bringing? You really don't have a girlfriend? What a great opportunity. I'd bring a girl if I were you. I'm sure she'll be impressed when she sees you taking care of business."

Yang Zao turned and ran downstairs as fast as his legs would carry him, as if none of this would happen if only he could stop himself from hearing it.

In the dimly lit, desolate evening, the jagged black shadows of trees added to his sense of unreality. His head hurt so badly that he wanted to rip it off and toss it to the ground. The pain of this illness had given him the right to self-harm. Numb, he forced himself to keep walking — *relax, let things happen as they will, everything will be fine.*

II

Kaitai Restaurant wasn't the highest-class establishment, but from the outside it had a certain early 20th-century charm, and the corridor walls were covered with photos and autographs of VIPs and celebrities, some going back decades.

Yang Zao arrived fifteen minutes early. Yang Wan came on her own, bringing along Doudou. Mr. Qian and Ms. Xiao each brought a guest — the original plan was for all of them to make an appearance together, but the discussion was sidetracked by details such as who would go first, who would stand by whom, and on and on, and as they talked they drifted further and further from agreement, until in the end everyone just showed up whenever they wanted. Yang Zao preferred it that way. He wasn't happy about being trailed by a parade of hangers-on, and if a squabble broke out among them on the big day, they might not even make it through the door.

In the hallway, he ran into a familiar-looking waiter — Yang Zao had brought Mr. Qian and Ms. Xiao here once, and another time

Yang Wan had dragged him along to ask about the prices. Yesterday, Yang Zao had come again without telling anyone, and reached an agreement with the pudgy waiter. The bill for their room would be brought to him, and nobody else would pay a dime. This strategy was essential. With this simple act, he headed off the possibility that Mr. Qian, Ms. Xiao, or somebody else would suddenly get it in their head to pay the check. To win over Pudgy, he had put down a generous deposit of 500 yuan, accompanied by his ID card from the bus company. He knew his line of work was unlikely to impress, so he explained straightforwardly, "I'm just a lowly bus driver, and I don't often get the chance to take my friends out to dinner. I can't tell you how important this is to me."

He noticed that Pudgy seemed moved. "Don't worry. I'll turn away anybody else who tries to pay."

Since it was still early, instead of going directly to the room, Yang Zao went back to the end of the hallway and took a look at himself in the bathroom mirror. He'd thought of everything. He'd prepared a certain look to give to Brother Rong, and another to give to his men. He'd prepared two more distinct looks for Mr. Qian, Ms. Xiao, his sister, and the other guests seated around the table. Yang Zao rehearsed his repertoire of looks in the mirror, then wetted his hair and gave it a trim — suddenly he heard the sound of wind rushing in his ears, and his heart began to pound. He had the ecstatic sensation that he was floating off the ground. Damn, here it comes, he told himself. This is the biggest moment of your life.

Yang Zao approached the room, deliberately picking up the pace, and pushed open the door with a breezy, dignified air — the room was deserted, in disorder, cups half-filled with tea scattered all around, chairs pulled out, a crushed cigarette pack on the ground. He started. His ears began to ring. He must have gotten the time wrong, he must be mistaken on some detail. Or maybe Brother Rong just hadn't shown up! He went running through the restaurant, and after a desperate search finally found the pudgy waiter, who looked distracted and overwhelmed. It took him a moment to recognize Yang Zao. In a chiding tone, he asked, "You just got here? Your guests have moved to the grand hall on the fourth floor!"

The grand hall? he grumbled silently. The grand hall was no place for Brother Rong.

He was too impatient to wait for the elevator, so he bolted up the stairs. He heard the voices from far away. The grand hall on the fourth floor resounded with the clamor of cutlery and conversation, every seat filled, the guests done up in their most elegant attire. A few children ran helter-skelter while the women whispered back and forth and the men lit cigarettes for one another.

He must have made a mistake. This couldn't be Brother Rong's banquet. Yang Zao was getting ready to turn and leave when he heard someone shout, "Little brother, over here!" It was Yang Wan. She sat at a table in a far corner of the room, gripping Doudou's little hand, both of them waving. So he was in the right place after all!

Yang Zao's brain completely seized up. Luckily his arms and legs still worked, so he elbowed through the crowd and made his way to Yang Wan's table, bumping into countless people along the way, even slamming headlong into one woman's enormous breasts. The woman wore dark blue eyeshadow and a hip-hugging skirt. It took Yang Zao a few moments to realize it was Ms. Xiao. She pulled along a pimple-faced kid with his head buried in a cell phone screen. He guessed it was her son, the one who wanted to take the civil service exam. Beneath her makeup, Ms. Xiao batted her thick eyelashes at Yang Zao. The gesture came across as brazenly seductive.

Yang Zao felt his underwear getting soaked with sweat, as if he'd leapt directly into the mouth of a volcano. Yang Wan noticed him swooning and grabbed him a glass of water. "I had a seat at the main table, but the room got more and more crowded, and a fight broke out, so we had to move to the grand hall. After the switch, I couldn't get us good seats…"

Yang Wan talked and talked, and the flow of meaningless patter gradually calmed him down. He rose to his feet and looked all around. At last, among the faces in the crowd, he spotted the friend who'd brought him news of the banquet. He also sat off to the side, eyes darting here and there. At a more distant table, he glimpsed Mr. Qian. He cast Yang Zao a forbidding look, making it clear that he planned to pretend they didn't know each other. Yang Zao looked to his left and right, but Mr. Qian had no companion. What he did have was an enormous box nearly half his height which was wrapped in gold brocade and took up an entire seat. What did you know, Mr. Qian had brought a gift of his own. Displeased, Yang Zao turned his eyes away, and to his complete surprise saw Shushu sitting amid the throng. Dumbstruck, he immediately lowered his head.

What was Shushu doing here?

What kind of person was Shushu? It would be best to say that she wasn't a person at all, but an angel, a star, a rose. At the same time, she was like a cancer to Yang Zao, a curse of destiny that was eating him alive. He'd never told another living soul about his adoration for Shushu. He kept her locked inside his mind, a terminal affliction from which he gained a secret, morbid ecstasy.

This heavenly creature Shushu had suddenly descended to appear before him, leaving him gasping with astonishment. He restrained himself to just two more glances at her. Naturally, her beauty was of the highest order, but in no way was it overbearing or intimidating. She was gentle, mild-mannered, unfailingly polite, making small talk with every stranger who approached. Yet it was exactly this excessive friendliness that seemed to drain her, making her look old and weary.

Then it hit him, another wave of despair and torment, and his stomach twisted into knots. He felt something inside him had been trampled. He really wanted Shushu to ride on the clouds and the mist like the immortals of Chinese folklore, never to descend to the world of commoners. But now that he thought of it, if this dinner gave him the opportunity to help Shushu out of some kind of fix, he might gain more from the occasion than he ever expected.

Yang Zao steeled his nerves and managed to stop sweating bullets. Even if there were a few bumps in the road, he would press on with his plan. He was determined to make the banquet a success.

Yang Zao realized just then that there was nothing on any of the tables other than empty bowls, cups, and napkins. Yet none of the guests seemed to find this strange. Their gestures and expressions showed that they were relishing their parts in the unfolding drama, enjoying this grand occasion. Yang Wan was still blabbing on, but Yang Zao stood up anxiously from his seat and pushed back into the crowd of strangers, calling out to nobody in particular, "Sorry for the poor service. Let's get some drinks and appetizers on the table!"

A few glanced over at the man they assumed was the host, nodding and murmuring agreement. Others cast him suspicious glances, as if they could see right through this puffery. Pasting on a big smile, Yang Zao reminded himself again and again that among this sea of shifting faces were Brother Rong's friends and subordinates, and even Brother Rong himself.

Yang Zao called out for Pudgy, steeled his nerves, and issued a string of stern instructions. Pudgy passed on the instructions word for word to a few other waiters – two bottles of baijiu, two bottles of red wine, a pitcher of orange juice, two packs of Chunghwa cigarettes, and eight dishes of cold appetizers on every table. Pudgy gave Yang Zao a parting glance, showing apprehension, and even a bit of awe.

Yang Zao counted the tables. Two more had just been added. A few people still wandered around in search of a seat, like spectators arriving late to the theater. People continued to stream into the room from the elevator doors, some of them pulling along four-wheeled suitcases, as if they'd just gotten off the train, pressing into the crowd with expressions of blissful unconcern.

Yang Zao basically understood what was going on. For goodness' sake, even he, a city bus driver, had heard the news. Didn't that explain the problem right there? The precious news was like a big balloon, blown up by countless hopeful mouths until it was filled with flecks of spittle, growing bigger and fatter as his friend blew into it and passed it on to him, he passed it to Yang Wan, and she passed it to Mr. Qian and Ms. Xiao. Drawn by overinflated promises, everybody and his brother had shoved their way into this room. It was that simple.

He had two credit cards in his wallet. He could pay them off later, so he figured things were still under control.

Yang Zao walked from here to there, calling out for the waiters to set the tables and arrange the chairs. They rushed from table to table, making little adjustments, and the air was filled with the sound of tables and chairs scraping the floor. The guests stood up, then sat back down. He heard mumbled complaints and patient, polite explanations, alternating like the ebb and flow of waves.

Pudgy gestured ingratiatingly to Yang Zao. "Right now, if you could look down at this room from above, you'd see that the tables in the grand hall are arranged just like two plum blossoms. The table in the middle is the flower's heart, and the others surrounding it are the petals. The plum blossom is the city's official flower."

He pushed back through the crowd to Yang Wan's side. Doudou, who'd been crying out from hunger the entire time, now slept peacefully, sucking on his thumb, his face as peaceful as a little Buddha. Yang Wan was relieved. "I'm glad he's finally gotten to sleep. He needs his energy to meet Brother Rong. Oh yeah, when are you going to take us to see Brother Rong? We have to make sure we're at the front of the line. From the looks of things, he's going to be exhausted by the end of it."

"Do you think they're all here to see Brother Rong?" Yang Zao knew the answer, but still held onto a thread of foolish hope.

Yang Wan gave him a meaningful glance. "We can't be too self-centered. It just goes to show what a powerful man he is. Hey, I just saw Shushu over there. Forget it, I'm going to put away this crystal hairpin, there's no use now that she's here." It seemed that before the auditions were even finished, Yang Wan had given up on getting the part.

Watching her movements and her expression as she put away the hairpin, he felt hope slipping away, and he spoke the truth. "I'm not going to be able to push to the front. Even my friend has to wait for an introduction."

Yang Wan showed no sign of surprise, lowering her voice and saying, "Then we're not going to wait in line like a couple of idiots."

She drew closer, grabbed Yang Zao's shoulder and pushed, and they hunkered down as if lying in ambush in the jungle. "I'll watch over here and you watch over there. If somebody important shows up, we'll see the ripples run through the crowd. Keep an eye on Shushu. I heard Brother Rong used to like her. We'll let her hook him, and we'll reel him in." Not missing the opportunity for a bit of delicious gossip, she added, "I heard she got into some trouble, and only Brother Rong could help set things straight. I'm a little worried maybe he doesn't treasure her any more."

Having been assigned a clear task, Yang Zao felt his senses regain their sharpness, and he surveyed the grand hall like a 360-degree surveillance camera. Faces of every shape, size, and description hovered in a sea of cigarette smoke. The murmured conversations of the guests floated through the haze like captions on a TV screen. A man with a stubbly beard was exhaustively describing all the times that his motorcycles had been stolen over the past few years, his tone both prideful and indignant. "I've lost eight of them! It's like winning the lottery eight times, but in reverse. I know the thieves have to make a living, but it's not my job to feed them all. I'm not asking much. I just want Brother Rong to give them a talking-to!"

Beside him, an old woman with a swollen face broke in, disgusted, "Lost motorcycles? Brother Rong has more important things to do. I lost my grandson."

He saw two girls who looked exactly alike, one wearing a panama hat, the other with spiked studs dotting her outer ear. Panama Hat asked in a nasal tone, "Are you following me?"

Spiky replied, "Do you really think Brother Rong can get you that movie role?"

"You've got no business following me."

"I'm trying to help you. I heard Brother Rong only likes threesomes." Panama Hat silently wrapped an arm around Spiky.

Yang Wan's finger jabbed him abruptly. "Police. There's a guy behind us wearing a checkered shirt. After my divorce, he helped me change my residence permit. There's a big mole on his forehead — wait a minute, then turn and look." In a tone of panicky delight, she urged, "Remember what I told you. The mayor's a nobody compared to Brother Rong!"

Who gave a rip about the police? Yang Zao had just caught sight of a genuine celebrity, a guy who was always on TV talk shows. The TV personality wore an old tank top, and without his suit, he seemed to have shed the affable everyman image he cultivated on TV, which oddly enough made him seem much more normal. The crowd and the people clustered around the tables in the grand hall chatted, exchanged greetings, and told jokes, but behind all of it there was the feeling of something weighing on their hearts, a sense of disorientation, as if they were a herd of helpless lambs being dragged by invisible reins.

He got the sudden sensation, both bitter and oddly comforting, that he was not alone, that they were all brothers and sisters. Suddenly, a renewed resolve welled up within him, rising from the soles of his feet through his legs and into his abdomen and his throat, expanding into the grandiose conviction that he would be the savior of all of them. Let them all come, all the people who waited outside for Brother Rong. Let them come, from the main streets, from the alleys, from the slums. Let them come by boat, let them come on horseback, let them come bearing battered umbrellas, let all of them come from every corner of the city in every which way. Yang Zao would buy each one of them dinner, even if it left him penniless — for the last few years, he had muddled through life, directionless and powerless, but that wasn't the real him. Only now had he truly found himself, only now had he realized his power to do great things, not only for the Yang family, not only for Shushu, not only for Mr. Qian and Ms. Xiao, but for everyone, everyone in the whole wide world, wahahahaha.

Feeling tipsy, his vision blurred, his gaze drifted back to Shushu's table, and his heart nearly stopped. A man in dark glasses had appeared at Shushu's side, and he was leaning in toward her as if to whisper a secret, his mouth stretched as wide as a hippo's, nearly touching Shushu's ear. Yang Zao looked all around, but nobody paid any attention to the man in the glasses. With utmost caution, Yang Zao tiptoed around three tables, squeezing in and approaching Shushu from behind. The man in dark glasses was talking about how he'd gone to Mt. Jiuhua on the first day of Chinese New Year to make an offering of incense sticks, how he'd paid big bucks to be the first to light one, and how the abbot had told him that he was destined to meet someone important this year. Hearing this, Yang Zao pressed in closer. What was Brother Rong doing lighting incense sticks? What did he need the luck for, and what kind of VIP was he supposed to meet? He himself was the VIP.

Seeing as he'd already gotten up, Yang Zao decided he might as well make a trip to the men's room. A guy stood by the urinal shouting aggressively into his phone. "Get your ass over here! I don't care if your house is on fire. This is more important. If there are no seats left, you can stand!"

Yang Zao opened the door to a stall and went in. He pulled down his pants and his underwear and squatted down when he felt a breeze blow against his bare buttocks, then further up. It was cool, and it tickled. He reflected absentmindedly that the breeze in the bathroom stall was like the banquet itself, carrying with it a euphoria whose meaning was vague and indistinct.

The man with the cell phone left, and two others came in. They went to take a piss, and he could tell from their accents that they were from the north. "And you brought perfume for Brother Rong. Dumbass. Brother Rong doesn't wear skirts and doesn't have long hair. What makes you think Brother Rong wants your girly crap?"

"You're the dumbass. It's cologne, as in for men, as in for Brother Rong's men. Happy?"

"Fuck you, you moron! Don't you know that what Brother Rong likes is girls? You can empty your perfume right into the urinal." There was the sound of splashing, a flush, and then the men were gone.

So Brother Rong was actually a sister? And she didn't like men? They sounded like they knew what they were talking about, rattling on in their northern accents with the exaggerated r's as they talked about Brother Rong this, Brother Rong that.

Yang Zao stood up, stamping his numb left foot on the floor. It felt like his entire lower body had fallen asleep. He tried his best to recall any trivial bit of information he might have heard once about Brother Rong, but came up with nothing. The problem was that the Chinese word for "he" and "she" was the same, no way to tell them apart except in writing, and thinking of it now, although people were clearly in awe when they spoke of Brother Rong, he'd never heard any detail that would distinguish Brother Rong as a man or a woman.

What was he going to do now? The inevitable conclusion danced inside his mind like a hungry flea. As the evening wore on, his chances of meeting Brother Rong were decreasing by the minute. At first, he'd pegged the possibility at 100 percent, but as he ran into Mr. Qian and Ms. Xiao on the road, he knew his chances were falling steadily, like a glass ball dropping from the sky to the earth. Over countless evenings, it fell further and faster, so that by the time the banquet was moved from the room on the second floor to the grand hall on the fourth, it was just a few centimeters from the floor. Half a minute ago, with the unexpected revelation about Brother Rong's gender, the ball had smashed loudly into the ground, and with this came complete relief and freedom. He saw very clearly that the shattered glass ball had always been empty, and Brother Rong might well be a woman, or he might be nothing but a phantom hovering over this grand hall with its chandeliers, tables, chairs, and little vinegar plates, prepared for the arrival of nobody and nothing.

Yang Zao pulled up his pants and left the bathroom. Yang Wan was waiting by the entrance to the men's room, the sleeping baby's arms wrapped around her neck, a panicked look on her face. "Shushu got up and left all of a sudden with that guy in dark glasses. I was standing here holding Doudou, so I couldn't follow them."

Yang Zao absentmindedly comforted Yang Wan. In fact, he felt happy for Shushu and the man with the glasses. At least somebody got lucky today, he thought.

He took Doudou from Yang Wan and pushed back through the crowd toward the table. They hadn't been gone long, but it was long enough that two other people had claimed their seats. One of them had a blood-soaked bandage wrapped around his head and torso, and the other was a fatherly-looking man who was passing a scrap of paper from one person to the next.

"Scan this barcode, and it'll show you what happened to my son. Please, forward it to your friends, leave a comment, press 'like.' Or if you want you can curse me out, call me idiot, jackass, whatever." He gave a sad, stubborn smile. "We just want to make enough of a racket that somebody hears. I heard Brother Rong has an army of social media experts, ready to make any post go viral!"

Seeing that her seat was occupied, Yang Wan flared her nostrils, preparing to give the intruders a piece of her mind, but Yang Zao tightened his grip on her hand and pulled her toward the hall. In the narrow hall they crossed paths with a line of waiters who scurried along like soldiers in a Peking opera, nimble and steady on their feet, balancing plates one-handed. The food smelled delicious. Seeing this, Yang Wan called out in a small voice, "You ordered lobster? And sea cucumber? You'll be in debt for the rest of your life!"

Yang Zao shook his head. He suddenly knew what he had to do, and he pressed on. There was no time to wait for the elevator, so he pulled Yang Wan towards the corridor with the photos covering the walls. In a flash of understanding, Yang Wan quickened her step, sighing, "If I'd known, I would have taken a few more bites."

They could see that they'd nearly reached the ground floor, and once they did it was just a few steps from the staircase to the lobby, and just a few steps from there to the street, where there were buses. All they had to do was hop on one, and they could pretend none of this ever happened. Doudou, who'd been hanging all the while from Yang Wan's neck, had woken up and started bawling, and as they rounded the curves of the winding stairs, photos and autographs of celebrities flashing by in a blur, Doudou's cries reverberated through the stairwell, making an astounding racket. Yang Zao could see it now. Fourteen tables full of people ceaselessly working their chopsticks and chewing away at their food, all turning their heads at once to look toward the stairs.

Pudgy set off in hot pursuit, following the baby's cries as he rounded the corners in rapid spirals, chubby cheeks flushed red. He was obviously extremely flustered, and only when he caught up with them did he finally heave a giant sigh of relief. As politely as he could, he gestured for Yang Zao and his sister and the bawling baby to step into a small room that was halfway beneath the ground floor.

The room was covered in water stains and filled with discarded objects. The chairs were stacked nearly to the ceiling, and the legs of the tables intertwined in a chaotic jumble suggesting a variety of creative sexual positions. Pudgy's heaving chest seemed to be falling back into a normal rhythm, and he stared at Yang Zao through watery eyes.

Mortified, Yang Zao lied, "I was just taking these two home. Look, the baby wouldn't stop crying. I was afraid he'd bother the guests. We're not trying to get out of paying or anything."

Only half listening, Pudgy flashed an awkward, fake smile, pulling two things from his left pants pocket – 500 yuan and Yang Zao's work ID card. "I'm sorry, but I can't take your money."

Yang Wan had been doing her best to comfort Doudou, but at

this, she quickly perked up and reached out to grab the money and the card. Not yet understanding, Yang Zao just stared at Pudgy. With his other hand, Pudgy reached into his right pants pocket and pulled out yet more money. He kept digging and digging, coming up with more and more bills. His pocket was like a bottomless well of cash. As he put the bills on a couple of round tables whose four legs were hopelessly jumbled, the pile rapidly began to resemble a small mountain. It was hard to look away.

Pudgy explained apologetically, "You see how much money I've collected. Everybody was fighting to pay the bill. And not just the people in the grand hall. People were coming up from the first floor, the second floor, the third floor, and some of them even came in from outside, threw down the cash and left. People called up, wanting to pay in advance. Some of them transferred money into the restaurant's bank account, begging us to pay the bill for them. Some people even tracked down the owner. The owner threw a tantrum, saying it was his territory and he'd be damned if he'd let anyone else pay the bill. He went to the kitchen himself to order more food."

Yang Zao was at a loss for words. He looked all around him at the mold-covered walls of the basement room, the water stains and the chaotic mess of tables and chairs, and he thought he must be dreaming. "Well then, I'll have to buy dinner for Brother Rong some other time."

Yang Zao rubbed his hands together and smiled. He looked like an orphan again.

A SECOND
PREGNANCY, 1980

Translated by **Helen Wang**

The main reason for my mother's lowly status in the family, and for her poor relationship with my grandmother, was that my grandfather, my grandmother, my father, and my mother herself, had always wanted a boy. My family was not unique. This was what everyone wanted. Unfortunately, I turned out to be a girl. My grandmother doted on me, but the situation was far from ideal. My father had been the only son in the family, and there was the question of how to continue the Lu family name. My mother decided to risk having a second child, which meant going against the new national policy that "one child was best."

The year was 1980, and the family planning policy had just started. In rural towns, women (and the men behind them) were not really on board yet. They expected they'd be fined and that would be it, right? If a baby boy was born, then it would be worth it. What's more, my grandmothers' generation had all had five or six children each, and knew from experience all the "secret signs" that predicted the sex of a child – what it meant when the fetus moved at night or during the day, when the mother's belly was round or oval, when the mother could or couldn't bend forward, when the mother did or didn't get freckles, when the belly button did or didn't pop out, when the mother stepped over the threshold with her right or left leg first. If these "male" parameters indicated a seventy to eighty percent chance, then the family would quietly prepare to pay the fine and take their chances on having a son and grandson.

My mother scored highly all round, particularly the criterion "unable to bend forward because she's carrying a boy." She was a typical case, even down to washing clothes at the table. The chances looked good. But for her, the consequence would not be a simple fine. She was a people's teacher, a civil servant of some sort, and for civil servants, the killer move was suspension from work. This really happened, and not after the birth, but before. Almost as soon as the pregnancy was visible, she went to class one day and discovered another teacher standing on the podium. She was given orders to stop teaching.

At the time, the branch secretary of the production brigade was my grandmother's nephew, but family planning was such a high-voltage wire that he couldn't touch it. If anything were to happen, he'd have to step down. So he put on a smile and came to pay his respects to my grandmother and press cigarettes, Da Qian Men cigarettes, a good brand, into her hands, all the while affectionately calling her "Niangniang." My grandmother accepted the cigarettes and put them to one side, while she picked up her water-pipe, which gurgled as she inhaled.

Then the director of the local committee of the Women's Federation came, and the head of the school, and the head of the production brigade. We had a stream of visitors wearing down the threshold. Our home had never been so crowded.

Each visitor would weigh in with a new argument. My mother's teaching position could not be guaranteed — that was clear. Then there was my grandfather, the brigade's accountant, always called "Accountant Lu" about town. He spent every day on his abacus, doing the brigade's accounts, and often helping local people balance their books too. He was well-respected, and this work was an important part of his later life. But he would be dismissed as well, by association. "If you want a grandson, then you can't be Accountant Lu." The next step, they said gravely, would be to go to Nanjing, the provincial capital, and find my university-educated father, who was working as an engineer, a highly respected position.

And so on it went, with one step leading to the next, and the situation growing increasingly serious. As in war, it was building up to a climax, and the more dangerous the situation looked, the clearer things became. In reality, fighting for oneself or one's family against a production brigade and higher authorities meant there could be no reprieve. Defeat was inevitable. The only question was what steps were to be taken. All those home visits, all the "ideological work" was about marking out the steps. My family's honor, which they praised repeatedly and effusively, was for the large part exaggerated, and at the end of the day it boiled down to one thing. "Neither the Lu side or the Wang side of your family is a pure peasant family. Both sides have family members in high places, university students, members living off the public purse. In terms of awareness and outlook, there has to be a different expectation of you." The complaints carried on in this vein.

The whole family listened and worried, at first shaking their heads, then nodding. The initial excitement gradually gave way to the feeling that their honor was being seriously compromised, and they quietly acquiesced.

The defeat was not without honor. They could get through this, and it was something that all the neighbors could understand. They would not think the family had capitulated too soon, nor would they think that the brigade secretary had been unduly harsh towards his Niangniang. My mother's pregnancy was now at an advanced stage, and both sides discussed the details amicably. She would be treated well — at eight o'clock the next morning the production brigade's tractor would come to pick my mother up and take her to the town hospital to be induced. Another couple of pregnant women from a neighboring village would also get the tractor treatment. It was not easy for a production brigade to send a tractor like that, and these women were at different stages of pregnancy, but all of them agreed to take the "public transport" on the same day, in order to comply with and implement the "family planning."

In fact, the real reason why my family was willing to give in was not just because of the so-called "family honor" and the pressure of dismissal from public office. There was another reason, but the family was keeping it secret.

A few days earlier, my mother, now over eight months pregnant, was crossing the bridge when a midwife spotted her from the distance. The midwife went white with shock, then caught up with her and gripped her arm. "Ms Wang! It's incredible! The baby's turned round, and it was so clear. I saw it for myself. It's a girl!"

These midwives had a wealth of experience and had pulled countless babies from the birth canal. They knew all the secret codes and logical expectations relating to babies — you could say they had all the authority of an ultrasound. And that being the case, it was better to back down.

Everything pointed to one inescapable conclusion – that this "second pregnancy" would soon be over. But as dusk approached, a drama unfolded.

That evening, after seven and before it got dark, for some reason — perhaps because she was able to relax after all those days of stress, or because she was tired and upset about the imminent loss of the baby, or maybe because the Old Man in Sky decided to have some fun — whatever it was, my mother suddenly felt a pain in her belly, and soon after that, she began to bleed and her water broke. The baby came early. My feisty little sister, adamantly refusing to become a lump of flesh in the surgery of a rural hospital, had diced with death and come leaping and bounding into this world, a perfect, healthy baby.

But what a bittersweet world it was, and what a half-hearted welcome she received. If only she'd been a he! The atmosphere in the room was as cold as ice. My mother said she hadn't asked about the baby, but she knew from the deathly silence, from the way no one made a sound. The midwives were always right! Then she fainted. I was seven at the time, clinging to someone's leg, not understanding what was happening, and asking over and over again if it was a boy or a girl.

At eight o'clock the next morning, when the roosters and hens were up and the early-rising farmers were out on the land, the tractor came sputtering round the corner. With the engine still running, the driver craned his neck and yelled, "Ms Wang."

The neighboring women at the side of the road all laughed out loud, "Save your breath! She doesn't need to go any more! She's had the baby already!"

"What did she have?" the other women on the tractor asked in chorus, as though anxious about their own babies. The voices of the pregnant women trembled in the thin early morning mist.

As my mother had already given her word and had agreed to be induced the next day, it was decided the baby's early arrival was a case of force majeur. The authorities eventually issued their verdict on how the matter should be dealt with. The teaching position would remain hers, and she could continue as before as a people's teacher, but there was no denying that this second pregnancy had added a "heavy burden" to the nation, and therefore a fine must be paid.

"How much?"

"Fifty-six yuan."

Those years my mother earned 14 yuan a month, so that was four months' wages, probably equivalent to over 10,000 yuan today. The fine was considered fair. To this day we still tease my little sister. "Fifty-six yuan, that's what you're worth!"

When I think about it now, I can see that the matter was handled with a great deal of sympathy. The family was so unlucky, and there'd been so much anguish before finally agreeing to the induction the following morning. And after all that, it was still a baby girl!

If my mother had given birth to a boy, the situation might have been completely different. About four or five years later, one of our neighbors, a stubborn character, resistant to the end, was determined to have a second child, and his family's gamble paid off. They had a big fat baby boy. That year the family planning policy was at its strictest, and everywhere people were being hauled, and the authorities made examples of them. They were threatened with a fine of 2,000 yuan, a terrifying amount of money, but the family held its nerve and decided to name the child Shuangqian, meaning "Double Thousand." There was no end of pressure to remove this little emperor, but in the end, all their haggling was successful, and we heard that they were eventually fined a few hundred yuan.

Some people doubted that the Lu family's second child was really a girl. In those days, the local custom was to ask a nursing mother from another family to give a newborn its first sip of milk. It was called "turning on the milk." A mother nursing a baby boy would be asked to "turn on the milk" for a newborn girl, and vice versa. But there wasn't anyone nearby who was nursing a baby boy, so my family asked a mother who was nursing a baby girl. The woman was puzzled, and, while feeding my little sister, would slip her hand inside her clothes to try and establish the facts. My poor mother watched from the side, sadness welling up inside her. She wished she was lying.

My mother is a strong-minded person, but this whole business, this whole process, made her feel utterly useless and utterly desperate. Her eyes were red from crying every day, and she wanted to die. At the time, I was in second grade in the same primary school where my mother taught, and her colleagues, my teachers, would tell me to run straight home after school and look after her and help her to recover so she could come back to school as quickly as possible, as it was quite difficult to keep her position open. So I raced home every day, my book bag banging against my bottom. It was not long before my little sister started smiling at my mother. Eventually her tears dried, and her mother's smile returned. When her 56 days of maternity leave were over, my mother took the cradle to class with her. She didn't dare take another minute, in case there had been a mistake and she was not to be allowed to continue as a "people's teacher."

But the story doesn't end there. About seven years later, in 1987, my mother unexpectedly found herself pregnant again. By this time the rural family planning policy had reached a more established "mass base," and people did not hesitate, resist, or torment themselves over it. The whole family, young and old, was in agreement. They would not keep the child. My mother was very busy during that time with her pupils' graduation exams, and then with the family's fields. She put the induction off until she was over seven months' pregnant. By then certain details revealed quite clearly that this time she was having a boy.

The following year, my grandfather fell ill and died. The year after that my father fell ill and died. When my grandmother wept for her dead son, she said the same thing over and over – three men of the family lost in three years. It took me a while to realize that she was also grieving for my little brother who never came into this world. To her dying day, she wanted that grandson.

SPEECH: NEITHER PROUD NOR PREJUDICED

A SPEECH GIVEN AT THE CHINESE LITERATURE BOAO
FORUM ON NOVEMBER 3, 2015

Translated by **Shelly Bryant**

In recent years, in my contact with foreign copyright agencies or agents, I have encountered the same situation countless times, a sort of "customized theme" in their requests. One German agent contacted me and asked if I had any "contemporary" novels set against an "urban background." One Italian publisher asked me for "realistic" stories about "things that really happen," adding that it was better if it had a "strong narrative," while some others wanted stories "about young people" with "high information content." On these requests, they offer further explanations. One reason is that the earliest batches of Chinese fiction exported to the West were classics like *The Dream of the Red Chamber* and *The Water Margin* or local-color novels of the early founding days around the 1950s, and later, family novels and historical novels. They feel that today's foreign readers are no longer interested in these things. They are not able to identify with traditional rural fiction, so they want to read works about something "happening" in "modern" China. Secondly, to them, literature is an important way of coming to understand a country and, since China is less rural and there are large cities everywhere, they want to see depictions of that part of China and people's lives there. Thirdly, they ask, "How can your generation still write 'stylistically old-fashioned fiction'? Don't you all live in big cities? Isn't this what you are familiar with?"

Honestly, I do not like or agree with their views and analyses. Whether the story is set in urban or rural settings, ancient or modern times, and whether it is fiction or non-fiction are not measures of their literary merit. If we rely on these measures to determine whether we should translate or import a given work, it is erroneous, since it is too simplistic and arbitrary, and even goes against the very purpose of literature.

But somehow, it seems I have also come to understand and accept this situation. In the current exchange of international copyrights, China is clearly in the position of a seller, and the majority of American and European countries in the position of buyers. They have an eye for media hype and the ability to attract attention. The first thing they look at is sure to be the "theme" or "topic." They work hard to question, trying to dig out the core of a story. What kind of story is it? What is its most prominent feature? Does it talk about the deprived or the powerful? Is it a tragedy with twists and turns? Is it a story about some mysterious non-governmental influence? On and on they go. What the West looks for in Eastern literature is like a host welcoming a distant, unfamiliar guest, trying to size him up in a rough, rapid scan. It is a time-saving, quick view, tainted by the eagerness for instant benefits. They have not reached the stage of a heart-to-heart talk or pondering slowly over and digesting each others' words. A deeper, higher level of textual analysis and a more accurate judgment (on such literary aspects as aesthetics, innovation, and evaluation) might have to wait a long time. The host will eventually notice that in the heart of this weather-beaten guest are sweetness and compassion and a distinctive Eastern perspective of his land. From then, he can welcome the guest with ease, mutually exchange what the other needs, sharing literature, which is now to be found everywhere, like good friends— but there is still a long way to go to reach this stage.

My personal understanding of this process is that there is no room for arrogance. While biases may exist, we must examine the origins of these biases. Is it a matter of the sinologist's perspective and taste? Does it have something to do with the courage and insight of the publishing house? Does it rise from the expectations of foreign readers? Is it some kind of divergence caused by geographic or ethnic diversities? Is it out of people's well-meaning but desperate wish for exchange? Does it come from some inexplicable economic or geopolitical motives? Or is it the oppression of commercial forces or dominant cultures? There is much more analysis to be done, going well beyond the scope of my own abilities.

But I want to discuss what comes out of this, which is connected with the third point the foreign publishers have alluded to, their reason for making a purchase — the expectation of "our generation of writers." But that expectation is not just held by them, the foreigners. It is also found, more or less, among domestic readers, publishers, and critics, and even us writers ourselves. So what I want to say next has more to do with the second topic, namely, to question whether the writing of our generation has really walked out of the shadow of the long-standing local-color novels and entered into a so-called urban writing.

First, I would like to briefly explain the growth of our generation. Taking myself as an example, in the past, for thirteen years, I was an out-and-out country girl, messing around on the muddy soil of my hometown, then by passing a college entrance examination, I moved into the provincial capital, Nanjing, where I studied and have remained until today. A considerable percentage of my peers have a similar background, growing up in their early years in a solidly rustic environment. Sooner or later, usually by the age of twenty, we actively got involved with urban life and become interdependent. A Yi (阿乙), Xu Zechen (徐则臣), Sheng Keyi (盛可以), Cao Kou (曹寇), and others all fit this general description. From a mere statistical perspective, our scope of experience in the city has far exceeded that of the countryside. Of course, this experience will start to mingle with our childhood, reading, education, and association to produce complex physical and chemical effects, eventually seeping into our blood, constitution, bile, and DNA.

But on the surface, aside from the little Achilles heel, where there seemed to be a residue of the rural 1980s, like a muddy birthmark, with a hidden rusticity and easily resentful character, the remaining parts, from the slender lower limbs (for lack of physical exercise), from our typical mode of student speech, from our huge appetites for all forms of modern aesthetics, from our appeal to the so-called international vision, we have, as a generation — voluntarily, quickly, and precisely — become urbanized. This is not good news, but neither is it bad news. It's just news, and news we have no control over. A person is synchronized with her or his environment, and it is also true of the little town or village where we were born. It may have happily and crudely become urbanized, or it may be huffing and puffing its way on the road to urbanization or drooling over the scenes of an urban fantasyland. We and our homeland are both heading toward Rome.

With our Achilles heel, I am afraid we are, deep down, all still just kids from the country. Even a simple passing thought of the countryside will trigger in us inexplicable pain. We find it more engaging to quarrel in our local dialects in private, and we fervently want to eat crisp pickled melon from the countryside when we have a fever. But in any case, the steely body of the city is already beginning to cast a huge shadow over our novels, forming the background, the protagonists who act, the flavor, the dialogue, the conflicts and hopes, the values to be destroyed or built. This seems only logical, a matter of course, so urban literature becomes like a huge melting pot, with a fire burning ever brighter beneath it as the kindling is consumed, casting large, flickering shadows on the wall beyond. People rejoice, saying, "Urban literature has arrived! It has been harvested, heated, and served!"

But in fact, when it comes to urban writing, I have my doubts.

The city has a will and has its own character. For instance, it has its well-developed jungle laws of commercialism, filled with the luring splendor of Mammonism, and a social climate always at the temperature of zero degree. Its most revered gods are speed, efficiency, and technical know-how, and it is built on a speculative moral code. The city is a perfect field which simultaneously suppresses and purifies human nature. It glows with a kind of dazzling beauty like that of quenching gold, which results in a rebellion and correction of virtue, classicism, sophistication, and humanism.

But when our generation enters the world of urban literature, it seems we unconsciously bring the strong rural traditions that have nurtured us and sheltered us like the roof over our head. We always have a sort of pastoral sentiment and nostalgia for comparing the past with the present. With a sense of superiority because we are on the moral high ground, we tend to seek the warped, the repressed, and the incomplete, as the psychologists, sociologists or critics of human nature often do. We are always sentimentally attached to our homeland, have a sense of parity deep in our bones, see dilapidation and ignorance, slowness and backwardness as a sort of tone for old pictures, a sort of sadness, a decadent but "classical" beauty. And when we turn our sights to the city, a black veil always falls over us. Even if we acknowledge the city's strengths, its progress and advancements, and even if we have embraced and possessed each other, innately we are still nervous and overreacting, and hold judgment about the city with a feeling similar to that of The Second Sex – nervous and overreacting. The city is evil; the countryside is beautiful. What we see are the violation and harm of beauty by evil, the mutilation and substitution of the new for the old, like steel and concrete slicing humiliatingly and destructively through the soil and plants.

I think we are all like the photojournalist in the movie *Rear Window* who peeks at city life through a dark "rear window" located at a place where the city joins the suburbs. He uses the partial logic gained from his partial peeking to build up follies, drama, and criticisms. The minor flaw here is to what degree do we, who think ourselves clairvoyant and sophisticated, fit into such a huge city and develop empathy? Can we really participate in, become aware of, and see through the core of the city and its consciousness? When we present and build the city in our writing, is there a sort of moral arrogance and aesthetic prejudice hovering in the local background? Are there a definite "discriminating heart" and a "sense of orientation" and therefore a set of "limitations"?

Looking at contemporary foreign fiction, and Western fiction in particular, such as *Freedom* and *The Corrections* (Jonathan Franzen), *A Visit from the Goon Squad* (Jennifer Egan), *The New York Trilogy* and *Brooklyn Follies* (Paul Auster), *Ecstasy* (Ryu Murakami), *A Perfect Day to Be Alone* (Nanae Aoyama), or *Snakes and Earrings* (Hitomi Kanehara), I notice that they have a sense of belonging, an affinity to the city, an outpouring of gentle feelings, a natural display of chaste sympathy and affection in their works. They tend to identify themselves with the indifferent interpersonal relationship, the "blood and iron" rules, and the idea that all things decay fast. These gentle feelings are very similar to those we hold toward the classical and traditional countryside. Their whole life was thrown into the flow of the city from the day they were born. All their memories, communication, entertainment, and rules are derived from the hard core of the city. The city is their hometown. Perhaps authors born in the 1990s or the early decades of this century will be able to write in this way, but our generation cannot.

But again, this is what I most want to say today. This birthmark or Achilles heel, this limitation mingled with our pride and our prejudice, perhaps, is our generation's hallmark in turning to urban writing, and our characteristic and contribution. Perhaps it is up to us to faithfully reflect this generation, and society as a whole, with its particular context and process.

Ours will not be like Western novels, writing about the self-confidence, dejection, and apathy of old cities. The novels about burgeoning cities under our pen will be full of turmoil and vitality, full of entangled conflicts and ruptures. Our line of sight is tainted with the immaturity typical of drifters. We use a point as a reference for the whole surface. We take a part for the whole, using what we glimpse to nourish the imagination. Somewhat breathlessly, we take our all-too-short experience of the city and add it to our innate rural genes and inherited aesthetic, throwing in our acquired knowledge and mixing it all together to form a complex vision, projecting it toward a similarly complex, mixed city life to try to write of a city in the process of developing, even though that development is uneven or premature, resulting in many complications. This city is piled up in luxury and violently misunderstood. It becomes notorious, being vilified even as it is pursued. It is seen as a hotbed of evil of all sorts, but at the same time, it is seen as courageously and powerfully pulling this Eastern country forward at full speed, even including our always memorable rural civilization, which we believe is being destroyed by the cities.

From this perspective, I am now kind of convinced by the sort of "orders" and solicitations we receive from Western publishers and agents, those I mentioned earlier. Biased external expectations and our own biased limitations are like the convergence of pure and turbid rivers, which will eventually be the most telling hallmark of our generation. It is going to be different from the middle-class Western writing, which is mellow and stereotyped, arrogant and cold. With our fiery zeal, we will forge a complex, splitting, self-contradictory experience that is fresh, and that is only present in China, and only in the experience of writers of this generation who share that mingled urban-rural background. We will dive in as latecomers, deep into this age's belly, its iron and rust, and play our part in laying a huge cornerstone of Chinese literature.

ABOUT THE AUTHOR

Lu Min was born in 1973 in Dongtai, Jiangsu Province, and currently lives in Nanjing. Her mother was a teacher, and her father an engineer. At the age of eighteen, she began working as a post office clerk, a secretary, a journalist, and a civil servant before finally becoming a professional writer.

Lu Min started writing at the age of twenty-five and has published novels such as *Universal Love Letters, The Steering Wheel, Undeliverable Feelings,* and *Dinner for Six.* Her short story collections and novellas include *Accompany the Feast, Farewell Song, The Viewfinder,* and *Stirring up the Dust.* She has been awarded the Zhuang Zhongwen Literary Award, the People's Literature Award, the Chinese Writers Award, the Monthly Fiction Reader Award, and the Selected Fiction Award, and she was honored with the Lu Xun Literary Award in 2010. Her abundant literary achievements eventually made her the youngest Vice Chairperson of the Jiangsu Writers' Association and one of the Top 20 Future Masters chosen by The People's Literature.